BURSTING ALIVE

Healing your damaged emotions through your miracle journey to wholeness

By Jodie Smith

A Companion Book to Buried Alive

Seventeen expounded steps and exercises

Bursting Alive
Healing your damaged emotions through your miracle journey to wholeness

By: Jodie Smith

ISBN-13: 978-1725749917
ISBN-10: 1725749912

All scripture quotations in this book are from the New King James Version of the Bible unless otherwise noted.

Edited by Patricia Bollmann

For information, to schedule speaking events, or to order books by Jodie Smith, please communicate by email to **Jsmithstilllaughing@yahoo.com.**

Dedication

I dedicate this book to my faithful and dedicated husband, Scott. He has been my greatest encourager and supporter to keep writing and helping people through my miracle journey of healing. While writing this book, if I came to a point where I needed a little help with memories, Scott was there to gladly help me in any area he could. Thank you, Babe, for loaning me your sermon notes to use for my last chapter in this book, "You Are Valuable." The day I heard you preach that message God spoke to my heart about using that title for my last chapter. Babe, you are my cherished soulmate!

Comments

"Nothing is better for us when we feel we are in disrepair with emotional or mental disorders, hurts, or pain than to have some guidance and steps to follow toward healing in our minds. I think *Bursting Alive* might be the only book written by a former Borderline who wrote the steps of healing that she herself walked through to complete healing and victory. I encourage you to use these biblical and clinical steps (with the help of a qualified counselor). They do work and can bring you to a place of healing and deliverance." – Vani Marshall, MS, BCBC, BCPPC, Professional Christian Counselor, Associate Professor of Psychology, CLC

"If you would have told me three years ago that this book would be written by this author who is now healed and whole, I would have had my doubts. I marvel at the grace of God at work in the miraculous recovery detailed in her first book. Now, in this work, we have been given a proven prescription for healing from Borderline Personality Disorder." – Stan Gleason, Assistant General Superintendent, United Pentecostal Church International

"The honesty and transparency openly displayed in this book is incredible. One does not need a mental health diagnosis for this book to be relevant. Anyone who desires an enhanced relationship with God and their fellowman will benefit from this incredible work by Jodie Smith." – Richard Moudy, MSW

"Borderlines are oftentimes stranded on an island with only themselves in the middle of everywhere, desperately in need of open heart surgery. By 'heart' I mean one's core belief system—the innermost being. With God as the Master Surgeon, through Christ, empowered by the Holy Spirit, Jodie participated in His open heart surgery on herself. Her personal account of this procedure is her gift to Christ's community to help and be helped. I highly recommend the reading and gifting of this book to all." – Steve Mulford, BCPC Living Foundation Ministries

"This book is a game changer. As I read it, I realized that it not only has the personal stories from Jodie, but also the diagnostic tools for self-reflection. It is an aid in helping individuals come out of the 'fog,' but also helps to establish a new identity in Jesus Christ. I went through some of the exercises as I read, and realized some personal truths for me. If you haven't read *Buried Alive*, I suggest you start there and then read this book with honesty and openness. This book has the potential to change so many lives. I am thankful for the work God has done in Jodie Smith and her willingness to be used by Him to reach others who are hurting and in need of healing." – Phillip Darnel, Associate Pastor, Life Tabernacle, Canton, Missouri

Table of Contents

Foreword

I was a child who struggled with depression and an inability to break out of buried resentment that I held due to the death of my mother. I would close the basement door and in the subterranean dimness I would pore over my mother's funeral book and look through her pictures, reliving the pain of her death, the loss of her voice, and the lack of memories of her life. At the time, it was all I knew to do. There was no escape; there was no way out except to grieve, cry, and live in self-inflicted pain. Don't get me wrong; I had a loving and caring dad and stepmother. They were unaware of all my pain and sorrow as I held it inside. I was buried alive.

How did it all work out? My story, while differing in many ways from that of Jodie Smith's, was quite similar in that we both experienced the change factor of Jesus. Many of the examples Jodie found to work also worked for me. Through the love of a lifelong childhood friend, parents, a caring church, and Jesus, I became whole.

While reading *Buried Alive*, I could relate to some of the issues Jodie faced. As a fire chief, I'm accustomed to putting out "fires" and resolving possible disasters. Each of us can do the same for ourselves by putting out emotional fires burning down deep inside. Although once buried, Jodie found healing and identity through Jesus Christ. God broke open her grave of abuse and freed her from her grave clothes so she could open up her heart to love and relationship (*Buried Alive*, 92–93). This was achieved through repentance, forgiveness, restitution, prayer, and the Word of God. "But because of his great love for us, God, who is rich in mercy, made us alive with Christ even when we were dead in transgression—it is by grace you have been saved" (Ephesians 2:4–5, NIV).

Through her writing in *Bursting Alive*, Jodie is asking you to open yourself up and begin drawing out the wounds from the darkness, exposing them to the marvelous light of God. By using her workbook approach, you will begin to be honest with yourself and accountable to a process of healing. My prayer is that this resource will touch your life through the testimony of Jodie Smith. It is time for you to really live!

Ron Smith
Fire Chief
City of Rolla Fire and Rescue

Introduction

I hope you have had the opportunity to read my first book, *Buried Alive*. If you haven't, I highly recommend that you read it before beginning this book. The two books go together like peanut butter goes with jelly. I took you through my healing journey after being diagnosed with BPD (Borderline Personality Disorder) at the beginning of 2015. The journey was very long and painful yet exciting and rewarding. It was truly a miracle. In *Buried Alive* I outlined the steps of healing that I used in my healing process. However, in *Bursting Alive* I have tried to expound on those steps and bring you to a whole new level or dimension. I have broken the steps down and organized them in a style similar to a workbook. But *Bursting Alive* is not just a workbook; it includes good reading material as I walk through the steps with you. I want you to feel encouraged as you read the gentle nudges I give along the way.

I truly want you to succeed, recover, overcome, and be healed! I know with God's help you can achieve it because with God *all things are possible.* I also want to encourage those who have not been diagnosed with BPD but are suffering from any other disorder, addiction, emotional crisis, anxiety, stress, anger, worry, racing thoughts, or fear. The majority of the population, although not diagnosed with BPD, will suffer from one or more of these symptoms of BPD during their lifetime. These biblical steps of healing will work for just about any problem or setback you are dealing with currently or will deal with in the future because the Word of God works!

If you are unsatisfied with your life and realize a need to change your lifestyle and make better choices, this book is for you. It outlines a biblical and clinical method. Anything that is Christlike and Bible based is worth trying.

If you have already tried several different methods, medicines, and/or counselors without satisfactory results, I'm asking you to give this book a try. I believe and trust our God. If He did it for me, He can do it for you!

I will be your number-one fan as I pray God's anointing upon everyone who needs help and is looking for answers. I pray for all the hands that open this book and every eye that reads its pages. May God guide your actions and choices as you read, and may He richly bless you as I pray a blessing over you!

Chapter 1

Self-Awareness and Honesty

Self-awareness is a powerful thing. Have you ever seen someone's face when something finally clicks? They can see the solution—or maybe they're just recognizing the problem—not only in their head but it has settled down deep in their spirit. A smile comes across their face, or maybe an expression of dismay. But the good thing is now that they see it, they want to do something about it.

Have you ever made a decision thinking it was a great idea? I remember several years ago, I made plans to go see one of my sons and his family. I was thrilled at the prospect of the trip because my son and daughter-in-law were about to have their second baby and I was going to be present for little Gavin's birth. I regretted that I had not been there for their first baby, little Tessa. And I hadn't seen them in a very long time. Needless to say, after paying for the airline ticket and making all the arrangements, I was horrified to realize that the very week I was scheduled to be gone, one of my other sons and his wife would be welcoming their second daughter into the world. This son lived only twenty minutes from me. This stuff happens when you have a large family—five boys and one girl. Needless to say, I flew to Connecticut for the birth of Gavin and my husband was home for the birth of Gracie. You see, there are times when we think we have everything covered but are totally unaware of how flawed our decisions are.

For many years I was held in the thralls of Borderline Personality Disorder (BPD), and when self-awareness came to me, it hit with devastating force. I finally realized what I had done, and I was greatly distressed. This new self-awareness compelled me to look back and identify my decisions or actions, some of which were done intentionally, others unintentionally.

Lack of self-awareness robs us of the things we need to develop psychologically in a healthy way. Damaged and dysfunctional, we have been walking in a fallen world for so long that it has become the norm for us. We just accept that we have no control and therefore have no power of choice. When we feel profoundly helpless, we begin to lose the sense of pain, which leads to the loss of a sense of self. This then leads to the loss of judgment.

I learned through personal experience that abused children have no clue that their home life is abnormal. They may be unhappy at times, but generally speaking there are usually some good and fun times even in the worst circumstances. By the time these children have gone through adolescence and reached adulthood, they have crammed all their bad memories and abuse into a deep, hidden compartment in their mind. This causes them to view the world through a clouded lens, and they base all of their decisions on this misshapen view. In order for God to bring us to self-awareness, He has to shine a light strong enough to penetrate through our thoughts, feelings, and our clouded lens.

> *Self-awareness hit me with devastating force. It compelled me to look back and identify my decisions or actions, some of which were done intentionally, others unintentionally.*

Many times adults will deny that they grew up in an abusive home. They might say, "That's crazy. I wasn't abused." But if they are honest with themselves, they need to call it what it really was. Only then can they deal with it. That in itself is a process.

Are you totally honest with yourself? Jennifer thought she was, because, she reasoned, if she wasn't honest with herself, then what she was telling herself was a lie—and, as she often said, "I don't lie!" However, when she began to have some self-awareness, she saw all kinds of ways she had covered up so she wouldn't have to deal with herself or her past. Many people have buried their past so deep that they have lost it and can't find the gravesite. We are lying to ourselves when we refuse to dig up our past. The only way we can ever go on into a joyous and prosperous future is to deal with our past.

Dr. Erik Erikson, a developmental psychologist, theorized that people progress through eight stages as they grow psychologically from a baby all the way to senior adulthood. He developed a chart to simplify these stages, and we can use it to understand where and what went wrong in our development. This gives us opportunity to think honestly about our own development and recognize at what age our abuse took place. In my own experience, I found that studying the chart made it easier to understand and accept what went wrong at a particular stage in my development. If this happened to you, it doesn't mean you were a bad person. It simply means that something did not go right in those particular stages of your life, and you suffered the consequences.

For me, stages three through six were a cloudy, mixed-up maze. I was sexually abused from ages four through twelve, and also dealt with many other unhealthy issues during this time. Later, at age twenty-eight, I went through a divorce. The early developmental issues skewed my whole learning structure and hindered my ability to communicate. I did not know how to solve issues and problems by talking through them. I had missed the part where I was supposed to learn right from wrong. I didn't know how to set good, healthy boundaries. Instead, I had learned that feeling good and being happy came through physical touch and emotion. Even as I entered adulthood, I did not understand that goodness and happiness came through my identity in Jesus Christ. I didn't even know my identity.

When I look back through these years of my life, I cringe. Only the grace and mercy of God kept me at many critical points in my life. As you read the above paragraph, I'm sure your mind began to wander through the corridors of your own life. I want you to take a good look and identify the things that seemed to go wrong. As you look at the developmental stages listed below, you will be able to see why you made some of the decisions you made. By going through the stages of your life and realizing what you missed due to abuse, bad decisions, health issues, or other factors, you can then begin to find some answers for your behavior.

For example, the consequence of my early childhood abuse was that I did not have strong boundaries in my teenage years. I didn't even know what the boundaries were supposed to be. This inability allowed some to take advantage of me. I didn't know when those boundaries were being crossed and didn't know if I was supposed to feel guilty or if what was happening was normal. In some ways I felt it was wrong, but I was confused because that's all I knew. It's what I had learned as a little girl.

We will follow and learn what was taught to us, not what was right and what should have been. This is why children of alcoholics will grow up to be alcoholics and will suffer the inevitable destruction. That's the only way they know how to be since that's the only example they saw. I'm not saying this is an excuse. We must at some point take responsibility for our actions and seek help and healing.

Each of Dr. Erikson's eight stages affects the growing child and the adult he or she will become. Failure to receive the proper examples and experiences at each stage can cause psychological harm. Each stage builds on top of the other, so if or when the damage starts, it accumulates. See www.psychologynoteshq.com/erikerickson/ for a graphic of the developmental chart.

1. Basic Trust vs. Basic Mistrust (infant–18 months)
2. Autonomy vs. Shame and Doubt (18 months–3 years)
3. Initiative vs. Guilt (3–5 years)
4. Industry vs. Inferiority (5–13 years)
5. Identity vs. Role Confusion (13–21 years)
6. Intimacy vs. Isolation (21–39 years)
7. Generativity vs. Stagnation (40–65 years)
8. Ego Integrity vs. Despair (65 and older)

The degree of success we have passing through each of Dr. Erikson's stages determines where we are in our adult maturity. As you can see from stage one, mothers have a heavy influence on whether their children develop a sense of basic trust. We are unable to go all the way back to our baby stage and take a look at what happened, but if our parents were going through hard times, it most certainly affected us.

For some adults, it's very hard to take an honest look at how our parents affected and influenced our lives. I believe that most parents try to do the best they know how, but life can deal some cruel blows to families. Maybe a physical illness took its toll and the parent(s) lost his/her job. Maybe the parents got stuck in some other unfortunate circumstance, and no matter how hard they tried to shield their children, they suffered and got hurt. Hopefully, the problem was dealt with in a healthy way, but sometimes it doesn't work that way. Dr. Erikson describes what it's like when an infant is wrapped in the blanket of basic trust: "This trust forms the basis in the child for a sense of identity which will later combine a sense of being 'all right' of being oneself, and of becoming what other people trust one will become" (quoted in *The Angry Heart* by Joseph Santoro, 17).

Sadly, so much damage has been done to some people that they are not aware there is a healthy and whole person inside of them waiting to burst out. I am a case in point. The person I was several years ago bears no resemblance to the person I am now. I have become much stronger in my decision-making and choices. My level of trust has been greatly altered for the better.

Below is Erik Erickson's "trust chart." As you look at it, think about the level of trust you have in other people. For instance, a child who grew up in a dysfunctional home does not learn anything about basic trust. This not only affects the person's trust level, it affects their identity. Someone like this cannot love properly or receive love from someone else.

How much basic trust do you have for others? How would you rate this on the following seven-point scale?

1	2	3	4	5	6	7
Basic Trust					Basic Mistrust	

In the space provided below, name some unhealthy methods, patterns, or words that played out in your childhood home. To help jumpstart your memory, I will give you an example of my own parenting style. When my children were young, I disciplined them according to my emotions rather than the circumstances of the offense. I would mete out punishment because my children upset me rather than match the punishment to the moral wrong they had committed.

1. _____

2._____

3. _____

4. _____

Are there any unhealthy patterns you have named above that you have picked up and are currently doing? We will pattern our own parenting style after our parents' style because that is all we know.

Name some of these behaviors on the lines below.

1. _____

2. _____

3. _____

If you have a graveyard of past abuses buried inside, there's no way you can raise your children in a healthy environment and make all the right choices for them. If you say otherwise, you are lying to yourself. You are covering up something you don't want to deal with. I'm not saying you will be a bad parent, but if healed you could be a much better one.

I cannot go back and re-raise my children. They are all grown. No, I wasn't a bad parent; I just did as most parents do—the best I knew how. However, if you have an opportunity to be honest with yourself and go through the healing process before you begin raising your children, both you and they will be better off. Getting that self-awareness early is always the best and healthiest way.

Had I achieved self-awareness early on, I could have been a much better wife to my sweet husband. I wasn't a bad wife, but many unfortunate situations and circumstances could and would have been avoided had I known I was struggling with BPD.

Only God knows our hearts. "For the word of God is living and powerful, and sharper than any two-edged sword, piercing even to the division of soul and spirit . . . and is a discerner of the thoughts and intents of the heart" (Hebrews 4:12).

God is well aware of places in our hearts where we have put up a sign that says "closed." It is a place where we secretly blame other people for our struggles and circumstances. I'm not saying that abusers should be let off the hook; they are guilty. We have all been wronged by people who have no excuse for their behavior. But at some point as we become mature adults, we must take responsibility for our choices and actions and develop some self-awareness so we can begin the process of righting the wrongs.

The relentless pain of the soul is another factor that stymies self-awareness. A victim will try continually to cover or block the pain. I know this because I did it. It is a coping mechanism in order to survive. The problem with that is when all of your pain is blocked, you don't experience other pains you should be feeling. Without realizing it, you have blocked out everything revolving around that pain and erected walls around all feeling and emotion. You view and register every action and feeling according to what is locked inside your heart. All of your responses issue out of your past experiences. That's why it is vital to take an honest look at everything that has molded you throughout your life and made you what you are today.

> *For the word of God is living and powerful and sharper than any two-edged sword, piercing even to the division of soul and spirit . . . and is a discerner of the thoughts and intents of the heart. (Hebrews 4:12)*

A person's style of communication is important. The Bible says, "A soft answer turneth away wrath." While this is true, it may be impossible for some who have blocked all feeling due to childhood abuse. When communication takes place, whether question or criticism or some other interaction, our answer rushes through a channel of our past experiences. When we respond in a negative way, we will often blame them for our retaliation. We don't just all of a sudden become angry, impatient, or totally distraught. Our response has passed like lightning through our filter and erupts out into the open. Everyone's response is different because everyone has a unique filter.

For example, Teresa and Jane are standing beside a pool when some jokester comes up behind them and, meaning no harm, pushes them in for the fun of it. Teresa knows how to swim and loves the water. She laughs it off and has fun splashing and swimming. Jane, on the other hand, is afraid of the water because buried in her childhood is a near-drowning experience. When pushed into the pool, she screams and flails around frantically until Teresa realizes her terror and pulls her to the edge of the pool.

When someone has a chip on their shoulder, everyone knows it because they are so easily offended. What we cannot see is that they probably are dealing with a heavy load of baggage crammed full of past hurts. I used to be like that. It didn't take much to offend me. But I would hide it in public because I wanted to be liked and accepted by everyone.

People who are easy to offend are self-centered. The world revolves around them. They have no regard for the other person and how they must feel or what they're going through. All they know and care about is their own hurt feelings.

However, pain is a necessary ingredient in our lives. How would we know we need to change position or take action or see a doctor if we never felt any pain? They say a burn patient with third degree burns does not initially feel the pain because the nerves are damaged. But as this patient undergoes therapy and their body starts to heal, intense pain sets in.

I can remember taking care of burn patients while working as a CNA many years ago. As long as these burn patients were resting in their hospital bed with their burns soothed and wrapped, they would do quite nicely. But upon taking them for a ride to the Physical Therapy Department they would cry out in agony with every bump they felt. As they were lowered into a tank of water and all the dead tissue was debrided by a scraping motion, they would cry or scream out in pain. As long as their wounds were left alone and nobody bothered them, they could survive. The minute their wounds were bumped or treated, they would cry out in pain. This is the way many have become emotionally. As long as no one touches our wounds of the past, we can survive, but please don't start digging deeper because it hurts too much!

As a pastor's wife for twenty years, I can remember talking with people, trying to help them manage their pain or problems. Everything was all right as long as we didn't dig too deep. But if we got close to the source of the pain, volatile emotions they didn't realize were there would resurrect, and they would refuse to talk any more or try to deal with it. They couldn't handle the pain it caused and were unwilling to endure it in order to work their way back to emotional health. Some people in all honesty don't want to be fixed. Or they are afraid that what they have felt all this time is a lie. They can't face that they are harboring a wrong perception of their past. They can't stand to look at both sides of the story. People don't like to eat their words, and believe me, I've had to swallow many a bitter mouthful. But God's grace helped me to digest them all!

How does a person numb their pain? With dishonesty. They have convinced themselves it didn't happen and will deny it. They pretend they had a great childhood just like everyone else. They live in a make-believe world. Who are they kidding? Not themselves and surely not God! Honesty is having the courage to see reality without conscious distortion, minimization, or spiritualization. Honesty begins when a person admits they were deceived and are willing to subject themselves to the searing light of truth.

Why is it important to admit the truth? Because dishonesty—living in denial—is an attempt to dethrone God, to shut Him out of one's life. It's much like a child who says, "You must play by my rules or take your bat and ball and go home!" In order to deny the truth, we must construct our own world. We come up with our own set of rules and guidelines. But God does not play by our rules. Therefore we make a life without God and learn to live without hope and love.

Dr. Dan B. Allender, in his book *The Wounded Heart*, writes, "An honest heart that embraces the internal damage will at some point be face to face with the memories of past abuse. The experience will be similar to holding onto the ends of a live electrical wire that burns and sears the soul, shaking it and transforming it into an altered, alien state."

Knowing this, it is understandable why an individual does not want to face the truth of their past when it involves some horrible abuse. In order for them to be willing to be true to themselves, the pain to remain the same must be greater than the pain to change.

I want to insert a memory here that might relate to someone who has not accepted the truth about their life. Years ago, my life was devoid of self-awareness and honesty, but I simply didn't know it. A person with a disorder or addiction does not live and move in the real world, so my conversations with others would go astray or end up in a morass of misunderstanding.

A healthy person lives in a world of honesty and reality. A conversation between a healthy person and an unhealthy person does not mesh very well. This is one reason why you see arguments; there is no communication because each party is playing by his own set of rules. Greg, the healthy person, wants Allyson, the unhealthy person, to see the truth as to why she behaves the way she does. Allyson wants Greg to give her a break and overlook her behavior. When Greg is unable to do that, Allyson feels isolated and thinks nobody understands her. No one is willing to see the point she is trying to make.

This scenario played over and over like a broken record before I was healed. I used to get frustrated and furious. My thoughts made perfect sense to me, so why couldn't anyone else see it? Why wouldn't anyone agree with me? I did not realize that I had BPD and would flip-flop from one side to the other side of an issue so frequently that I rarely made any sense at all. I was living in a world of pretense, where I could run and hide. I felt isolated because what I was feeling and saying was not real and there was no way anybody else could even begin to understand where I was coming from. It is impossible for someone to have compassion and concern for you when your feelings and thoughts are based on lies.

Only when Allyson unpacks the baggage she is carrying and takes an honest look at the contents (comes to grips with the truth) will her communication with Greg begin to improve. Then both of them can discover the reasons behind Allyson's problems and begin to deal with them. This is a true miracle for a person diagnosed with BPD. It is extremely hard for them to see the truth and then to face reality and live in truth. This is why the condition is called "borderline"; a Borderline's thinking hovers on the border of what they believe is or isn't true, and they can flip one way or another at any given time.

As Joseph Santoro states in *The Angry Heart*, "I want to be accepted by you, but I can't accept myself." Things will improve when they begin to drop the excuses and reasons for their behaviors, accept that they need to change, and start taking responsibility for those changes. This is the only way it will work.

The Borderline needs intervention and a supernatural touch, because a Borderline will glimpse the truth from time to time but within hours or days will slip back into false reality. I did this all the time. I would get to the point where I understood the truth in what was said, but it wouldn't be long until the battle in my mind would resume. I would mistrust the person that communicated with me. Were they trying to get at me? Were they taking everything into consideration? This is where I would begin to flip back and forth between the real truth and what I believed to be true. What I felt was so real to me that it was hard to believe the actual truth of the matter. For this reason alone it is a miracle from God that I am healed. Thank You, Jesus!

I want to take a moment to discuss addictions. Most addictions start because people are trying to cover up their pain. They don't want to deal with the memories and past abuse, so when the memories flood in, they turn to food or shopping or work or the demand for perfection. Maybe they rush off to the bar. Or their mind and/or body tells them they are hurting so they turn to the medicine cabinet for some prescription pain relievers. That's what a person's body does when it's addicted: it cries out in pain for another dose of "medicine."

This is one reason why it's hard to come clean with drugs because you really do hurt. And while you're swallowing the pills or drinking the alcohol, you are blaming someone else for your behavior. It is all their fault. They are making you do this to yourself. If they only knew what they were doing to you!

Maybe you're an individual who doesn't like to drink or take drugs alone; it makes you feel better to do it in a group setting. Does it justify your addiction? Does it make you feel better to go to a bar and see all the other unhappy people drinking away their problems? The only consolation I can think of is that they could say, "See, I'm not the only messed-up one in the world!"

Then there are the quiet ones who practice their addictions in secret. They might even be an apostolic minister, a minister's wife, or the spouse of a long-standing deacon in the church. No one has any clue how lonely, miserable, and full of pain they really are.

Maybe you practice cutting (self-harm). This type of addiction is more common than people want to believe. Actually, this is one of the symptoms of BPD. It feels good when a Borderline sees the blood flowing out of their arm or leg; they see it as a release from their inner pain. This can be very dangerous and leave lasting scars.

If a person chooses not to feel the pain, they are in reality choosing not to be alive. They are, in effect, buried alive. By the grace of God I was in the small percentage of Borderlines that did not have an addiction, but I knew people who did. I would get calls day and night when they were in a drunken stupor. It was so sad.

In lieu of an addiction, my coping mechanism was, when I reached a peak in a BPD cycle I would clamber into my car and drive, with tears streaming down my face, until I found a quiet, dark place to park. Then I would scream out to God for help. I didn't know what I needed; I just knew I was out of control. I do believe this is the reason why I did not have an addiction: I cried out to God for help instead of turning to substance abuse. Unfortunately, I was acting like a beggar standing on the corner, rattling a tin cup in people's faces. I was expecting—no, demanding—that God should come and help me. I had to learn to open my heart and life to Him in order to receive divine help. Openness is having a humble spirit, not a demanding attitude.

Honesty is the commitment to see stark reality and to turn away from your own invention of reality. When you are hungry for honesty, you must become humble and willing to listen as truth is spoken, no matter how much it hurts or affects you. You are willing to go past self-justification of your former actions and excuses. You want truth!

There is no working through anything or reaching out for help if you can't admit there's a problem. By admitting you need help, you are saying, "I will do whatever it takes to get through this. I will open up and talk and discuss things I hate to talk about." You must understand it's important to go back to your childhood

> Search me, O God, and know my heart: try me, and know my thoughts: and see if there be any wicked way in me, and lead me in the way everlasting. (Psalm 139:23–24, KJV)

and look at some things that weren't right. Most people who are suffering in their adulthood are doing so because as a child they experienced abuse in some form or fashion. Not only must you admit there's a problem, you must be willing to step outside of your comfort zone and into someone else's "box" and listen to them. You must listen as your family or friends explain how your actions, behaviors, and attitudes have affected their lives.

Contradiction and inconsistency are hallmarks of people with BPD. They are a defense mechanism in order to cope with all of the pain in their lives. Have you ever been around someone who constantly changes their mind? Are they inconsistent in their behavior? Do they have a hard time following through with everything? I struggled tremendously with this. It is very hard for a Borderline to keep a promise or follow up on something they promised because the only entity in their world is "me."

When your world starts to become "us" instead of "me," you are then stepping onto the pathway of honesty. It is a path others have winnowed before you, because you are beginning to understand the many things they had to do or avoid doing in order to live at peace with you.

After reading these last few paragraphs, I want you to begin to recall what others (family, friends, coworkers) have had to do differently or rearrange because of your attitudes, behaviors, and maybe even your threats. You might tell yourself, "I don't know what they are." But I guarantee that if you will think back, you can remember what they have said out of frustration with your actions. I will help you by naming a few of the comments I heard before my healing from BPD.

1. "It's like I'm walking on eggshells, not knowing when your moods are going to flip."
2. "You are requiring that I be perfect at all times—and that's impossible."
3. "You're so touchy I don't dare express any disappointments or concerns having to do with you."

No matter what disorder or addiction you have or even if you are coping with some emotional issues, your loved ones and friends are sacrificing. I'm sure you have heard them say many times what they have to do in order to make you happy. If you do not believe what they are saying or think they are exaggerating, remember they are saying how they are feeling, and that is what matters—not what you think they should feel, or how they should take what you dish out.

List a few of these comments on the lines below . . . and be honest.

1. _____

2. _____

3. _____

4. _____

25

5. _____

6. _____

I realize this exercise has been difficult for you. If you are willing to change and want to be healed, the first step up is engraved with the sign, "Self-Awareness and Honesty." Before anyone or even God can begin to help you, you must admit the truth about yourself— not just how you see it but how the ones closest to you see it.

Opening the door to honesty requires strength. But let me tell you that honesty will always bring hope, although you may not see the hope right away. You probably will feel so overwhelmed that you might want to turn and run away from hope. But I encourage you to keep on walking with your eyes fastened on the truth. Once you escape from the fantasy and grasp the truth, there will be hope and healing for you!

Look at it as a new beginning in your life. You can do this! Yes, it most likely will open up old wounds from the past, but as they say, "No pain no gain!" If you want to make a new start and get what you need from the Deliverer and Healer, you must acknowledge the truths in this chapter. You must say and/or write what the problem is. It's like going to the doctor for an illness; you must tell him what is hurting and where in order for him to help you get back to a healthy you.

Our God is a miracle worker! He specializes in seeing things that are not as though they were! Start seeing yourself the way God sees you, with a brand new, sound mind. A mind in which emotions are not exaggerated and stretched out of proportion. A mind capable of communicating in a healthy fashion and doesn't rely on an addiction to get you through the day. For me, hope welled up when I heard my counselor, Vani Marshall, say, "Jodie, when you told me and also recorded, 'I have BPD,' I knew you were on your way to your healing!"

I want to close this chapter by saying I believe in you! I am writing this book and offering these exercises because I know God can do all things. Your case is not too complicated for God to heal and turn around. God did it for me, and He will do it for you.

In this last exercise, I want you to write down any addiction, personality disorder, emotional disorder, or anything you might be suffering from. It might take a little space to write it down, but that's all right. When you write it down and admit, "I have _____, that's a great start. Just ask God to help you begin a new journey.

1. _____

2. _____

3. _____

4. _____

5. _____

6. _____

There may be more than one thing you are struggling with. That's all right too. God has you in the palm of His hand. He wants you to become healthy, healed, and whole. So, with a deep breath and great anticipation, let's move on to chapter 2. You can do this!

Chapter 2

Choosing Your Counselor and Support Team

For many children in grade school, recess is the highlight of the day. Fifth-grader Gus was chosen to be the softball team captain. That was the coolest thing! Gus wanted his team to win, so he tried to decide which kids to choose. He thought, *I need to pick the best players first, before the other captain chooses them.* So he chose the kid who could hit the ball out of the park, the kids who could catch fly balls, and the kids who could run fast. Last but not least, he chose the kid who could slide into home base. Gus could hardly wait until the game started. He was proud when the whole team came together and played their very best. Everyone on the team wanted to go home with a win under their belt!

If it was important to pick a winning team in grade school, it's even more important to pick a winning team to help you walk through your healing journey. I believe in you, and you're going to win. I know if you have accepted the truth about yourself and worked through the exercises in chapter 1, you are serious about achieving your healing. You are on a mission; you have begun your journey. Choosing your counselor and support team is a very important part of your journey. You supporters will be the ones who are willing to make a sacrifice and walk with you through the next season of your life. Your team should have at least four components:

1. God. God has to be the center of it all! When God is at the center, He will be your refuge and strength.

In God is my salvation and my glory: the rock of my strength, and my refuge, is in God. (Psalm 62:7)

I know God is not walking in flesh on the earth, but you must learn to talk with Him and lean on Him as if He were standing next to you in the flesh. This might not be new to some of you, but it was new to me. During my healing journey, God and I became best of friends.

29

Let's think for a moment. We all have been through hard times, mountains we've climbed with a family member or close friend. You don't forget those times because you were drawn very close to the people who were walking with you. They were right there when you needed them. They were only a phone call away. They laughed with you and cried with you. They shared your moments of grief and sadness, the moments that you hope no one will ever hear about or even ask about. They shared sacred times as well as horrifying times when you lost all hope and they had to talk you out of ending it all. They encouraged you and gave you hope that you could make it! I remember those times, and I'm telling you that God became that special Someone to me during my healing journey. He was closer than a brother!

> A man that hath friends must shew himself friendly; and there is a friend that sticketh closer than a brother. (Proverbs 18:24, KJV.)

God and I became best friends! I told Him absolutely everything about myself. Yes, I know God knows everything whether we tell Him or not. However, it's very important that we tell God everything about ourselves. This helps with self-awareness and honesty and also helps to heal our brokenness. There is so much that we don't know about our own hearts. David said, "Who can understand his errors? cleanse thou me from secret faults" (Psalm 19:12, KJV). Jeremiah said, "The heart is deceitful above all things, and desperately wicked: who can know it?" (Jeremiah 17:9, KJV). *Wicked* is a pretty strong word, yet there could be wickedness in our heart without our knowledge. That is why we need God walking by our side. He is an expert at inspecting our inward parts.

We pray, "God, please help me to understand what's going on!" when we should be praying, "God, I know that You know what is in my heart and mind. Give me a revelation of what's going on, in the name of Jesus." We must pray with sincerity and faith, knowing He has all knowledge. He is the Creator. He formed us in our mother's womb. Get excited about God! He will deliver you and walk with you through this healing process.

Without God on your team, you will not make it; conversely, if God is on your team, nothing can stop you or even stand against you

(Romans 8:31). You need to remember that when you are doing right and walking with God through the process and following your support team's advice, God is for you! It does not matter who is against you. Guard against listening to your carnal man. Instead, claim the promises of God in Scripture and believe He will give them to you.

> Being confident of this very thing, that he which hath begun a good work in you will perform it until the day of Jesus Christ. (Philippians 1:6, KJV)

God is going to complete the work He has started in you. You might be tempted to think God will give up, especially during the times He has to wait on you to make the right decision or choice. You may veer off the course. Look at the apostle Paul, who said, "I have finished my course" not "I have stayed on my course." You are human and will sometimes veer off course. But it's important that you get back on so you can finish your course! While walking through the healing journey, there are going to be good days and bad days. That's to be expected. Just don't quit during the bad days; keep the faith and finish the course. There will be days you would rather not remember. I have a pile of days I choose not to remember. Instead, I choose to remember the many days of victory and God moments, times when I didn't know what I was going to do and God stepped in and saved me just in time. "I'm gonna praise His name!" So veering off is not the problem. Be sure to get back up and move on. The bad days make the good days look *really* good!

What are some areas you need to work on to better your relationship with God?

1. _____

2. _____

3. _____

4. _____

5. _____

2. Your Pastor. You must walk under the covering of your pastor! This is vital. He is your shepherd. Anytime you get out from under the covering of your pastor, you are wandering out from under God's covering. This is dangerous. God shows your pastor things you cannot see. He sees the wolves when you don't. He cares deeply for your soul. God talks to him about you.

I am being very transparent in telling you my BPD wouldn't let me trust anybody. I had a wonderful pastor and shepherd. He was there for me and watching out for my soul, but I got scared and ran from him, thinking in my Borderline mind that my pastor wasn't making the right decisions. He couldn't do anything to save me from running except stand there and watch me run while the wolves chased me into the sea. Waves crashed over my head. Water drenched my eyes and I could not see. I could not breathe! Oh God, I grieve when I think about that horrible decision I made that almost cost me my life and soul. I'm sure my pastor prayed for me many hours that I would somehow see my damaged emotional sickness and come to my senses.

When you are misaligned with God and your pastor, nothing else will line up either. It's like trying to build a house on an uneven foundation. The house might look solid and secure as the months and years go by, but then you start noticing cracks in the walls because the structure is sinking unevenly. Yes, you can patch the holes and cracks. You can dab them with mud and plaster and paint. But the repairs will last for only a short time. The only way to fix the problem is to go all the way down to the foundation and fix the structure from the bottom up. If your foundation is not on the Rock, it will not stand.

When God started talking gently to me, it took me several months to line up. But eventually I went back to the firm foundation in Christ Jesus, and I aligned myself back up with my pastor. Doing that reunited me with my beloved husband. They were both waiting patiently for me to make some right choices. My pastor welcomed me back into the fold. I could not have asked for a better pastor and shepherd who showered me with bucket loads of mercy. I had to dig down to the foundation and get everything rebuilt the right way.

I can tell you from personal experience that had I not rebuilt my foundation, I wouldn't have received the miracle in my life. Like the proverbial house, my house weathered some hurricanes and tornados. But with God and my pastor on my team, I was still standing when the storm had passed on.

> For where two or three are gathered together in my name, there am I in the midst of them. (Matthew 18:20, KJV)

Isolating yourself will not work. Isolation is dangerous. When you feel like you need some alone time, someone else should know where you are and what you are doing. This is because abandonment is one of the reasons people suffer from BPD. Thus, if you isolate yourself without telling anyone your whereabouts, you are setting yourself up for failure.

Pastors are called by God. They have a heart for people like no other. God has prepared them for "such a time as this."

3. Christian Counselor. A godly apostolic counselor is a must! Everyone's issues, disorders, and addictions differ, so the help of a professional counselor may be necessary to achieve healing. It is good to include your pastor as you search for the right counselor. He might know some things about them that you are unaware of. Once the choice is made, let your pastor and your counselor guide you.

I know that God can do anything; I'm a strong believer in miracles and healings. I myself am a miracle. In addition, I believe God has equipped doctors to help us in matters of physical health. Very few people have a problem with that. But they will start to squirm when it comes to dealing with mental health. Why is it that they place a great divide between physical and mental health?

I must qualify my statements by saying I am not in favor of going to a psychiatrist and being put on a regimen of drugs with no counseling involved. I do realize that some people need drugs to correct chemical imbalances and disorders that no amount of counseling will help. However, I know people who would rather take drugs to numb their pain and emotions instead of working hard with the help of God and a support team to overcome their problems. They begin by taking medication, and when it kicks in, they think they are getting better. But in reality, they are covering up valuable and genuine emotions because the drugs are altering their thinking patterns. Borderlines already have issues with staying focused in the here and now, so adding drugs to that only makes it more difficult to

33

learn how to think properly. That's why I say it is very important to engage with a Christian counselor. I know this because I experienced many God moments in sessions with Vani. Vani used a lot of therapeutic exercises with me, but when God would come into that room and we felt His glorious presence, I knew He was doing a work that only He could do.

We are in constant conflict with Satan because he wants to take control of our minds. It is doubly important for a Borderline to realize this and also that there are tormenting spirits. I know because I had to deal with them myself. If you have a counselor who is sensitive to the Spirit, there will be a healing flow from the throne of God in your sessions. I also want to encourage you to keep attending church services with your heart and mind open at all times to give God a chance to work. I felt Him touch my mind during church services many times.

Nobody likes to hear how much something is going to cost. Counseling sessions are not cheap, but I assure you they will be worth every dime you spend. It will cost you anywhere from one- to two-hundred dollars per hour. In my experience, people don't take things seriously unless they're paying for it. So if you are investing financially in counseling, you are more apt to invest the work it will take to be set free from your addiction or disorder.

Returning to the subject of physical health, you have no problem paying for necessary surgeries. Many times your medical bills will mount up. Yet you—and possibly those around you—may squawk when you have to pay for your mental and emotional needs. In my quest for healing, I had to fly to Louisiana a couple of times to see Vani Marshall. Other times my husband and I would drive down there. Yes, it takes money and time, but you have to get serious and make it a priority. Once you take the plunge, you must decide there is no going back!

I am convinced that I had the best professional apostolic counselor in Vani Marshall. I would highly recommend her to anyone no matter the addiction, disorder, or other problem. I will go so far as to say she saved my life. Yes, God was my Healer, but a good counselor who can guide you along your journey toward healing is invaluable. BPD is a complex disorder, and you will need all the help you can get. Vani does telephone counseling and internet counseling as well. She resides in Alexandria, Louisiana, and attends the Pentecostals of Alexandria pastored by Anthony Mangun.

4. Spouse, Parent, or Close Friend. How old you are and whether or not you are married will be the determining factor in choosing a close confidante. My closest supporter was and is my husband, Scott. Vani advised Scott on how to react to me and what to do and say. This is vitally important. If you get the wrong person or someone who wants to help but doesn't know how, this could cause major problems. Living with a Borderline or with anyone fighting an addiction is not easy! This support person has to be very healthy, both emotionally and mentally. If they are dealing with past baggage, it would be wise for them to get counseling as well. Bottom line, you need someone around you most of the time. They must be willing and able to sacrifice their time and patience. Supporting you will drain them down to the empty mark. When a Borderline reaches a peak or a bad cycle time, that special support person has to be able not to take anything personally, but to let it roll off their back and move on.

Scott deserves a gold medal! My crisis peaked in 2015, and I walked out and stayed gone for about eight months. During that time Vani diagnosed my BPD and had some sessions with Scott, instructing him what to do and say when I had "moments"—or hours or days! He had to be strong and stay that way while he dealt with everything. Together, we were determined never to go back.

That dark time was bad. I lost almost everything that was valuable in my life. In fact, I may never regain some of the relationships that were lost. But God in His mercy helped me to make my way back. With my husband knowing how to deal with me and my BPD, we made a home all over again. We had to start from the ground up.

Scott was amazing! I have never seen so much love flow out of one man. He was there with me in the depths of my despair when I finally realized the immensity of what I had done and the mess I had made. He has been there to cheer me on and show-and-tell the milestones in my progress. He has been my shelter in the middle of the storm. He sacrificed everything. There aren't very many men who would take their wife back in and nurture her as lovingly as my husband did. We have gone literally to hell and back together, but now we have a great marriage. If we could do this, so can you! I believe in you!

Chapter 3

Your Family and Friends

Your family is a very important part of your life. Family and friends can either make you or break you. This is especially true if you are a Borderline because you have issues with maintaining healthy relationships. Many times Borderlines do not see they are associating with the wrong people. It is hard and maybe impossible to recognize and get close to healthy people when you yourself are so unhealthy. You have to decide, with the help of your counselor, pastor, and the person you have chosen to walk closely beside you, which family members and friends are safe to come alongside you in your journey toward healing. If you have family that do not understand where you are and where you are going, they may be a hindrance to your healing journey, so limit your time around them and do not discuss your journey with them. You don't need the discouragement they may bring you. Surround yourself with your support team and family and friends that will hold you up and encourage you.

You may have been disappointed in the way your family has reacted. Some family members will refuse to take part in your journey. They may not believe in you or acknowledge the validity of your diagnosis. Maybe your parents will deny there is anything wrong because their pride has gotten in the way. They want the "Perfect Family" symbol to remain intact. Then, unfortunately, there are those who don't even acknowledge the need for mental health. They declare, "It's all in your head!" Curiously, they are right. The battle takes place in the mind, and it is as real as if you are fighting cancer. These kinds of family members can totally sabotage your efforts toward healing, so it's best to limit your interaction with them.

Family relationships can get very sticky, especially if one—or more—has been your abuser in some form or another. If you're still living at home with your family, you're going to have a whole other set of issues and guidelines to follow. You may not be able to limit your time with family members who have abused you or still are abusing you. They certainly will not be interested in supporting you.

37

Instead, they probably will say things to anger and upset you. I would suggest that you find a room in your house that you can make your own space. It could be your bedroom or another room. If you don't have that, get creative. If you don't drive, find a peaceful place in your yard—maybe under a tree or out on the deck. Somewhere you can go for a while to rejuvenate your mind. You need a designated safe place.

If you are a young adult or older and have your own place or live with a roommate, you too must make some changes. Take into account your diagnosis and carefully choose the family and friends you will be close to. You have the advantage of gathering your belongings and leaving if you feel you are around someone or someplace that is unhealthy for you.

For those who are married, having children to cope with can be very difficult. I look back on my years of raising six children and realize how tough it was. One of my hardest battles was fighting depression. I wonder how my children and I ever survived. In a house with children there's so much noise and activity it is hard to find that safe place in your house where you can go to rest your mind in peace and quiet. Grab a few minutes when the children are napping and the house is quiet. If your kids are old enough to take care of themselves, they need to understand you need your space and some quiet time. Your husband will be a great asset to you if he is supportive. You must create an environment that is conducive to healing.

By now you are aware of your "triggers," things that set off your anger or maybe a sound or smell or event or someone's words that conjure up awful memories. It could even be the place where an event occurred. It is so much better for everyone involved if your family and friends are aware of your triggers and learn how to avoid them. Before I started my healing journey, I had no idea what triggered my reactions. Even if I thought about it after the fact, I couldn't figure it out.

Let me share one of my triggers. Growing up, I did not feel very smart and I struggled with low self-esteem. As an adult, if someone spoke to me in a condescending manner, it would trigger the thought, *They make me feel like a child again*, or *They think I'm stupid*, and I would get angry. Sometimes the trigger was as simple as someone explaining to me how they wanted the laundry folded, or when and in what condition they wanted a borrowed item returned, or what ingredients they wanted me to get for a certain culinary dish, for example. After I did the task, they would ask, "Now why did you do it like that?" For me there was no such thing as constructive criticism.

Now that I've shared one of my triggers with you, can you think of some that you struggle with? You may find, as I did, that it makes you feel better to write them down.

1. _____

2. _____

3. _____

4. _____

5. _____

6. _____

Again, it is important that everyone around you knows and avoids your triggers so you can begin to heal in an environment that's stable and consistent. Two of the most important things a Borderline needs are stability and security.

A Note to the Caregiver

You must work to produce a stable, consistent routine that will contribute to the Borderline's healing. Lack of stability and security will throw them from pillar to post. I know this firsthand. I loved being a pastor's wife of a growing church, but combining that role with BPD was difficult to the extreme, especially since I had no idea I was dealing with BPD. I was one of those pastors' wives that loved to host dinners and conferences, drive a bus route, teach a Sunday school class, and serve as music minister. I dearly loved all of it and will gladly do it again someday if it is God's will. But juggling all of those roles with BPD often spelled disaster. After the initial rush of enjoyment, BPD would rear its ugly head and I would decide I didn't like doing it after all. I would cycle and have a meltdown after each event.

A Borderline needs a "sterile" environment in order to heal. Think of patients who are put into an isolation room so they can recover from a serious infection. They are set apart for several important reasons: They cannot afford for someone to barge into their room, bringing with them a colony of germs that would compound their illness. They need a germ-free environment. People who come into that room have to wash their hands and suit up because they are there to help the patient heal. Only a few people are allowed in at once. Certain objects like flowers are banned from the isolation room. It is a very safe and sterile environment.

A cancer patient undergoing chemotherapy and radiation has to have a safe environment as well. Our youngest son, Austin, was diagnosed at age three with Hodgkin's disease, which is cancer of the lymph nodes. He underwent several surgeries, chemotherapy, and radiation. There were places he could not go because he was vulnerable to infection. He couldn't afford to be around people who were contagious. We had to rearrange our bedroom so Austin could sleep in his little toddler bed beside us. At any given time during the night he could get sick and need his mommy or daddy to scoop him up and run for the restroom. We were constantly aware of his every move and sound, and we knew what each one meant. This was a delicate time in Austin's life.

Looking at these examples, you can see why it is so important for a vulnerable patient to have a safe and sterile environment. Sending a very sick patient out into the real world could mean death. The same is true with a Borderline or someone with another disorder or addiction. They will not survive in the real world. It will eat them up. They need a safe, gentle place with people who care and who can observe what they say and do. It takes extended time and extra care for them to heal. They don't need someone spreading "germs" in their environment. They don't need anything that could cause a setback in their healing journey.

Name some family members that you feel are healthy and good to be around:

1. _____

2. _____

3. _____

4. _____

5. _____

6. _____

As you wrote these names down, I'm sure you thought about the other family members that you need to limit your time with. Name those below.

1. _____

2. _____

3. _____

4. _____

5. _____

6. _____

Now think about your family as a whole and how you relate to them. My point here is not to totally ban family members who won't be an asset to your healing. I simply want you to think about this and realize how important these choices are to your healing journey. Some family members will enhance your healing, and you are safe being around them all the time. There are other family members you have to watch what you say and do and limit the amount of time you spend with them. You must protect your environment as if it were a pot of gold!

Toxic Friends

Toxins friends are poisonous, so I'm dead serious about this. Ingesting their poison will make you sick or even cause death. I know that when family is involved you don't always have a choice about whom you are with, but you most certainly have a choice when it comes to friends. There are friends you picked up along the way that were toxic to you, but you didn't know how much danger you were in. Borderlines have a hard time with relationships anyway. They tend to bounce around from friend to friend. In my case, it was easy for "friends" to take advantage of me because I had never learned to establish good, healthy boundaries. But as soon as I started the healing process and became aware of my BPD, I had to make some hard decisions.

You see, sometimes friends can be so toxic that you just have to burn the bridge and never look back. This is very difficult because the friend won't understand why you're making the break. For example, let's say you have confided many things about yourself to your friend Karl, but he doesn't believe you have a problem or a disorder. You've been on such familiar terms with Karl that it becomes impossible to maintain the status quo and still be friends. Then there's an additional complication. As a Borderline, you have blamed Karl, along with many others, for all of your issues, so when you turn around and tell him the true reason for the breakup, the situation becomes impossible. Furthermore, Karl is probably carrying his own heavy load of baggage and if you try to maintain the friendship, he will become a serious hindrance to your healing. Your main focus has to be on your healing and what's best for you. You cannot seek to please your friends because it will only lead to disaster, and you will sink back into the same old muddy quagmire of problems.

If you have a hard time with relationships, here are some true, life-changing statements that will help you. After you've read them, maybe you can come up with some other statements that would be of particular help to you. Read through these every day to remind yourself it is possible to have good relationships!

1. I can learn to trust without fear.
2. I can love without getting hurt.
3. I can set my own healthy boundaries.
4. I can enjoy being with people that I love.
5. If I can love, it will replace the fear.

Can you name a few statements of your own? Think of things that you struggle with and put a positive spin on them. I guarantee these statements will encourage you. Repetition helps your mind to grasp and comprehend the truth.

1. _____

2. _____

3. _____

You need a fresh start in order to heal. If you have an addiction, you simply cannot hang around the same crowd you once hobnobbed with. You have to set up a whole new circle of friends. It's time to get really serious about this. If you are ready to make a change for the better and move toward a new healed you, you will have to make some sacrifices; for instance, you may even have to drive a different way home from work. That may sound ludicrous, but it's true. There are some places you must avoid so you won't be thrown into a relapse of your sickened state. You must work out a new routine that will help you stay on course. If you really mean business and want a lasting change, you will figure out a system that works for you.

Name some toxic friends that you need to break ties with in order to heal.

1. _____

2. _____

3. _____

4. _____

It has been estimated that up to 69 percent of people with BPD become addicted to alcohol compared with the 9.5 percent addiction in the general population (Santoro, *The Angry Heart*). Further, it is all too common for BPD to co-occur with SUD (Substance Use Disorder).

A client with BPD and a co-occurring SUD presents some particular challenges. BPD is difficult to treat, partly because of the pervasive, intractable nature of personality disorders and partly because clients with BPD often do not adhere to treatment and often drop out of treatment. The impulsivity, suicidality, and self-harm risks associated with BPD may all be exacerbated by the use of alcohol or drugs. In addition, the presence of BPD may contribute to the severity of SUD symptoms, and the course of SUD treatment may be more complicated for clients who also have BPD. (*The Journal of Personality Disorders* [15, 416–424]; *The Journal of Abnormal Psychology* [106, (1), 74–84]; Substance Abuse and Mental Health Services Administration)

Can you see why I'm belaboring this point? If you keep contact with your former crowd, you will get sucked back into that lifestyle, and, if you are seeing a counselor, you probably will quit going. You have to sever yourself from toxic friends in order to survive, live, and thrive.

When I was going through the first several months of my healing journey, I kept a low profile. My husband was by my side most of the time. He looked out for me. He knew the things that bothered me and the situations that could set me back. We found it was best to keep a slow, steady pace. I know it might be difficult for some to do, but if you have to work, you at least need a fair amount of time to sit and rest your body and mind. I had to learn how to pace myself. If we had a very busy week or an out-of-town trip, when we got home I would purposely rest and not do much. It really helped.

Name some friends that would have a positive influence on you.

1. _____

2. _____

3. _____

4. _____

5. _____

6. _____

Nurturing Yourself

"Nurturing yourself means allowing yourself to feel good in healthy, not addictive, ways" (Santoro, *The Angry Heart*).

You must learn to nurture your inner self as well as the outer self; take good care of your mental and emotional needs just as you take care of your physical needs. For instance, you must be sure you are getting a good amount of sleep. And I don't mean two or three hours. They say a good night's sleep is really nine hours! It helps tremendously to go to bed at the same time every night. I know that might not be possible every time, but try it on the nights that you can. We set a bedtime for our kids, so it must be a pretty good idea for adults as well.

Do you know that while you sleep your brain produces serotonin? Serotonin impacts every part of your body, from your emotions to your motor skills. Serotonin is considered a natural mood stabilizer. It's the chemical that helps with sleeping, eating, and digesting. Serotonin also helps to reduce depression, regulate anxiety, heal wounds, and maintain bone health. So if you're not getting enough sleep, you are being deprived of all the benefits God designed for you through rest and sleep. Psalm 127:2 says, "It is vain for you to rise up early, to sit up late, to eat the bread of sorrows: for so he giveth his beloved sleep."

I heard Dr. James Hughes say once that a lady came to him for counseling. The lady was delirious and confused, so he immediately asked her how much sleep she had been getting. She said she hadn't slept in three days! He told her she didn't need any pills. What she needed to do was go home and get some sleep. She did, and the problem was solved!

Lack of sleep really does hurt your body. Further, it is a mistake to make decisions in a sleep-deprived state. It has been said that driving while sleep-deprived is the same as driving while intoxicated. If you want to conquer BPD, an addiction, or any other problem, you must allow yourself enough rest, sleep, and relaxation.

Another important area of nurturing yourself is to eat sensibly. Don't consume foods and drinks that you know will adversely affect your body. If you know certain foods will keep you up all night, avoid them!

Weight loss is a big deal in our society. People are always kicking themselves about losing weight. Yes, it is good to keep a reasonable weight, but don't go overboard with it. I have seen many people start out on a special diet and lose weight like crazy. The trouble is, once they lose the weight, they return to their old eating habits, regain the weight, and soon they are back at square one. This weight cycling, sometimes referred to as yo-yo dieting, is detrimental to your body. It can lead to high blood pressure, high cholesterol, and gallbladder disease. It also can have negative psychological effects.

I do think many people turn to food to relieve stress and pain, some to the point of addiction. Pentecostals are notorious eaters; it is what we do for entertainment! In my studies with Light University, they recommend that a person should "eat healthy" without calling it a diet. It is better to watch your food portions. It is a slow, sensible way to lose weight instead of trying every fad diet that comes along. Fad diets, in my opinion, do more harm than good. It is a proven fact that if you eat right, you will feel better; if you feel better, you will be able to manage other areas of your life more efficiently.

In my opinion, eating right is all about self-discipline, a skill some of us just don't have. We need self-discipline in every area of our lives: eating, sleeping, and relationships.

Making long-term goals regarding weight loss helps you to see beyond the here and now, to glimpse the person you desire to become. Don't be unrealistic, however. Take it a day at a time. Remember it is not a race; you are not competing with anyone—at least you shouldn't be. If you have a close friend who will join you in healthy eating and exercising, that's great. It's nice to have someone to encourage you when you're tempted to do or eat things you shouldn't. But it can be very discouraging if you compare yourself to someone else. The only person you need to compare yourself to is God.

Finances

One more thing to set you up for a promising start is to get your finances in good shape. If they are already in order, that's great! But this is a difficult area for many people, and financial troubles can cause much stress in your life. If you can't seem to control your spending, if you can't cover all of your bills, ask for help. There are agencies to which you can send a lump sum, and they will organize and pay your bills for you. Or if you have a trusted friend who is a good financial strategist, let go of your pride and ask for help. There is no shame in it. There are many people with valuable talents that would love to help.

As I close out this chapter, I want you to think of six positive facts about yourself and write them down. This exercise will encourage you. I believe in you, and I want you to believe in yourself! Here is an example of what I would write: (1) I am a positive person. (2) People say I'm pleasant to be around. (3) I have a sense of humor. (4) I love God and try to serve Him to the best of my ability.

1. _____

2. _____

3. _____

4. _____

5. _____

6. _____

Chapter 4

Daily Journaling and Encouragement

Journaling is a great idea, and it will help you tremendously. Look at it as your recovery or healing journal. Make it an exciting activity of your day. Try to choose the same time each day to write in your journal; make it an important part of your routine. Invest in a really nice notebook and put some dividers in it to section it off. This journal is going to be more than just your day-to-day experiences; it will include a lot of personal information so put it where only you have access to it.

Give yourself enough time to write because recording your thoughts, feelings, and memories can be a slow, painful process. Many memories are stashed in the hidden recesses of your mind, and it will take some time to pull them out. There will be days when the words will flow out like a river; other days you simply can't articulate your words. When I first began journaling, I would be thinking of a particular event but just couldn't put it into words. If this happens to you, don't stress. In due time it will all come to you and you will be able to sit down and let it flow. Remember you are writing about some of your deepest pain. Don't worry about how your writing sounds. The grammar, spelling, and punctuation don't have to be correct. Your journal is just a private place for you alone to express and write what comes to you.

> *Studies have shown that the emotional release from journaling lowers anxiety, stress, and induces better sleep.*

Journaling will free you from some of the emotions that are weighing you down, and it will disentangle you from mental traumas. It will give you a therapeutic outlet—emotionally, physically, and psychologically. Dr. James Pennebaker, author of *Writing to Heal*, has even seen improved immune function in participants of writing exercises. He explains, "When we translate an experience into language we essentially make the experience graspable." Studies have also shown that the emotional release from journaling lowers anxiety, stress, and induces better sleep.

Journaling will also help you during your counseling sessions because it reveals what you have been repressing and your counselor can then get at the root of your problems. Remember there are no right or wrong experiences, memories, emotions, or feelings. Don't think that what you are writing is confusing or misleading. Instead, it more likely will become a source of encouragement to see how far you have come. When you're having a bad day, take a moment and turn back the pages a month or two. I have done this and have been greatly encouraged.

All self-help books present their ideas about journaling, but here are some of my suggestions:

Childhood Years

Your first section will consist of musings about your childhood days. Think back as far as you can and record any major events, good and bad. This exercise is very important to your recovery because most of the time your reactions and responses stem from your childhood. You may not think about it at this point, but as you progress in your healing, it will benefit you greatly to be able to go back and read your childhood memories.

For example, let's say when you were little you got lost while exploring in the woods nearby and panicked. Years later, you're driving along, take a few wrong turns, and soon you don't know where you are. Terrible panicky feelings arise. Heart pounding, you think, *This isn't like me. Why am I feeling and reacting this way?* Those feelings are emerging from that small child within.

I have found that any event, circumstance, or place that stands out in a person's mind has significance because their mind can't let it go. Here's what I mean: As a child I suffered with feelings of inadequacy. Everyone seemed to treat me like I couldn't do anything by myself. Nothing I did ever seemed to please. In addition, I couldn't process my thinking. If Mom gave me a task that included two or three steps, I would begin and then get lost. If she told me again and I still didn't get it, she would have my older sister step in and do it. I'm not saying this was right or wrong, but it would cause me to think, *Yay! I got out of doing that!* Then, as I got older and people would explain how to do something the least bit complicated, I found myself feeling like an inadequate child: "Get me out of this! I can't do it!" And I would get upset because I thought they were treating me like a child.

In your journal, record any nicknames you had. Write about the death of someone in your family. Write about the effects of witnessing the adults in your life going through a divorce. Tell if you were raised by both parents or a single parent or even a grandparent or guardian. Were you in foster care? Were you adopted? Were you homeschooled or enrolled in public or private school? Be sure to add events that happened to other family members that affected you and altered your life or lifestyle.

Recording these facts and many more will help you to open up and be totally honest with yourself. You can express yourself freely because your journal is for your eyes only unless you choose to share. As you begin to write about the events from your past, you will find that feelings will rise to the surface, some you didn't even know were there. As you continue to write, your mind will begin to unveil more memories. Don't attempt to close off these feelings; they will be of great therapeutic value to you. My counselor, Vani Marshall, would tell me, "When you cry, those are healing tears." That's why I say when you start crying while talking to someone on your support team or writing in your journal, you have hit the spot where the pain is.

Write down some experiences you had as a child that stand out to you, both good and bad:

1. _____

2. _____

3. _____

4. _____

5. _____

6. _____

Teenage Years

Many unfortunate milestones are passed in the teenage years: some have tried their first alcoholic drink, drugs, or cigarettes. Others attempt suicide or engage in promiscuity. Some run away from home. Some with driver's licenses accumulate traffic tickets or wreck their cars. Girls are sometimes violated on date nights.

For many, these years are lonely years. Some teens feel as if they don't fit in with the group. A lot of bullying takes place. I personally hated school when I was a teenager. I felt lonely and had very few school friends.

Is there anything you did as a teenager that you're ashamed of and nobody knows? Your journal is a perfect place to write about that and get it out of your system. You're not the only one who had trouble during this stage of life; the teenage years are hard for everyone. Your mind and your body are changing and maturing. You're trying to figure out who you are and what you want to become—then you keep changing your mind. I remember that as a teenager I always wanted to be older than I was. I never could just stop and "smell the roses." I was always wishing for things I couldn't have. I was lucky in that I had an older brother and sister who would graciously take me with them to join other teenagers. Wherever there was a party, that's where I wanted to be.

If there was a time I could do over, it would be my teenage years. I made so many mistakes, the worst of which was failure to pursue my calling. If I had had a pastor or mentor at the time who got involved and guided me during those years, things might have been better. Yet I was in such a state I'm not sure I would have listened to a leader during my teenage years. I didn't feel any self-worth or self-respect, and I certainly didn't feel valued by anyone. However, looking at my teenage years from another angle, I see those as my "grace" years. God protected me so many times when I could have been destroyed. God, in His mercy, saw me not as I was, but what I could be!

Write down how you viewed life as a teenager:

1. _____

2. _____

Write down how various circumstances in your childhood changed or affected your teenage years.

1. _____

2. _____

3. _____

Day-to-Day Events and Feelings

This section can be used for writing about experiences and feelings as you go through the day. Doing this helped me tremendously because there were days along my healing journey that seemed like pure hell. I would think desperately, *I just can't do this anymore!* Those are the days you must pick up your journal and turn to an account of a really good day when you conquered the world. You nailed it! All of your days won't be bad. Some days will flow smoothly like the current of a river. The grassy banks will be lush and green and you are on your game. Remembering days like this will give you hope and encouragement. You can turn to those pages and see in black and white when you made it. You triumphed over that negative voice you were hearing. You defeated the rage that was boiling up in you.

There will be days you just don't feel like journaling, and some days your schedule will be too tight. That's okay. Just be sure you write at least three times per week. When you're writing, include exactly how you feel about everything. If someone said something to you that really upset you, write about it. If you feel at the moment that you hate someone, put that down. It's very important to use the best words that describe your feeling and emotion at the time. I mention this because, as you are writing, you will see how this particular feeling was the result of a certain action, and this action was because of what that person said. It is very interesting to discover the split-second connections that are made in our minds as we navigate through life.

Sometimes as you are writing, revelation will come to you. When you notice recurring actions and feelings, you start to recognize a pattern. It then gives you something tangible to work with, to share with your counselor. I hope by now you see the value of journaling. Without it, days slip by in a blur and end up in the cloudy mist of memory.

Triggers

Triggers are both a blessing and a curse. As we discussed in the previous chapter, everybody's triggers will be different because everybody has different life experiences. One of my major triggers was when someone got angry or upset and flew out of control. When this happened I would dissociate—disconnect from the present context and retreat into a make-believe world. A tempestuous, emotional atmosphere would make me freeze in my steps because of certain situations that happened as I was growing up.

Some of your triggers are obvious. You know immediately what it was and why it triggered your emotions, and oftentimes affected your whole demeanor. Other triggers are very subtle, and you may not even know they are there. Then maybe something will click and you realize, *I'm not tracking right. My thinking is off, and I feel "out of body, out of mind."* I have recognized many of these subtle triggers. This was a vital area in which my husband's support contributed to my healing. He could sense something was creeping up on me before I ever knew it. He could feel my mood swings and knew when I was putting up a protective wall around myself.

A trigger becomes a blessing when you can look at it and realize it is telling you something is happening inside your mind and affecting your emotional responses. Triggers help you identify the things that have affected you over the years. They are there to tell you something is wrong so you can work through it. A trigger says, "You need to look into this, work on it, and fix it!"

I also believe that as you make progress on your journey, triggers will begin to fall by the wayside. The ones that still remain will become less severe. You will learn how to avoid as many triggers as you can, and when one does set you off, it doesn't take you as long to settle down inside.

You don't always have to know the reason the trigger is there in order to work on it. I will offer some exercises later in this book that will outline what you can do to overcome the triggers. Don't let them rule your life.

When my youngest son, Austin, was about three, he had a terrible experience. We were in my bedroom and I was sewing. As most three-year-olds will do, Austin became bored and wandered off to see what he could get into. He was playing in the kitchen when he found a barbecue grill lighter and discovered it had a little lever. I had not been able to get this lighter to work for several weeks, but I hadn't discarded it in the trash, thinking the fluid would leak out.

Austin worked the lever and a tiny flame shot out. He excitedly climbed onto a chair, and, working the lever, touched the flame to the ruffled hem of the kitchen curtains I had sewn just the day before. Unaware, I remained in the bedroom concentrating on my project, when the smoke alarm blared throughout the house. I jumped up and ran down the hallway, hearing the kitchen window break and shatter. I entered the kitchen only to see that my beautiful curtains were charred black and the fire was now beginning to devour the cabinets. I frantically looked for Austin while the smoke alarm continued to screech. My heart pounding, I finally found him hiding underneath his little bed. I dragged him out, scooped up fifteen-month-old Kaitlin from her nap, and rushed outside. Austin was so traumatized that he didn't speak the rest of the day.

This day etched deep marks in Austin's memory and became a trigger. If we were out and about and he saw anything that even resembled fire, he would run away screaming. This trigger remained with Austin for the longest time. If I was with him today and we encountered a fire, no doubt it would still silently trigger some emotion inside of him. Thankfully, Austin doesn't suffer from any kind of disorder. I just used this example to illustrate how an event or an experience can become a trigger.

Name some of your triggers:

1. _____

2. _____

3. _____

4. _____

5. _____

6. _____

If you cannot think of any, let me help you. Start writing down some things that people do or say that create a reaction in you. As you write, can you identify a connection? Do they all point to one main subject or theme?

As you identify your triggers, all of your responses and actions will take on new meaning. Your world will start making sense to you. You will no longer look at your emotions and think they don't make sense. Identifying and analyzing your triggers will become helpful to your healing journey.

The following self-help skill is my adaptation of "The Angry Heart Compass" outlined by Joseph Santoro in his book *The Angry Heart.* You can use this compass as a tool to help you determine which of the three zones you are in on your way to healing. Familiarize yourself with the descriptions listed under each zone: Borderline, Recovery, or Free Zone.

Borderline Zone:

Poor temper control   Mood changes
Addictive activities   Stormy relationships
Bouts of Depression   Can't trust anyone
Suicidal thoughts or actions   Don't know who you are
Anger, inconsistency   Racing thoughts

Recovery Zone:

Able to write about pain
Able to tolerate feedback without anger
Able to appreciate help
Able to cut short outbursts of temper
Able to cut back addictive behaviors
Willing to follow mentor's advice
Able to slow down stress-accelerated mind

56

Able to accept therapist's help
Able to accept your deficits without anger
Defensive wall is down more than up

Free Zone:
Able to openly discuss past pain with loved one
Words and actions are consistent
Able to hold on to close relationships
Know what you want from life
Able to laugh about and be at peace with your past
Can love another without fear
Can tolerate stress without resorting to addictions
Feel optimistic about the future
Can be affectionate toward loved ones
Able to hold steady employment

Studying this heart compass will help you judge about where you are in the healing process. If you haven't yet started your healing journey, you will see you probably have a long way to go. If you have an addiction or disorder, feel free to adapt the compass to fit your own situation. This will help you see what areas need work.

Santoro's heart compass really helped me through the healing process. I would go back to this page to determine the areas in which I had improved. Sometimes it seemed I had made very little progress. Remember you don't have to be perfect in every area. Just work on becoming better a little bit at a time.

One thing that helps is to try to eliminate the following three phrases out of your mind and speech: "could have," "would have," "should have." They will do nothing to push you forward. They will only discourage you and pull you back! As time passes, you will see yourself traveling from the Borderline Zone all the way into the Free Zone by the help of Almighty God! Always remember that healing takes time. It is like peeling an onion slowly, one layer at a time. Sometimes you will cry along the way, but keep working at it until you reach the Free Zone. If I did it, you can do it! Here are six reinforcers to help you keep a positive attitude:

1. I don't blame myself for being the way I am. It's not my fault.

2. I must realize I am the only one that can change myself! I must take ownership.
3. I want to change! I must!
4. I am striving to work on all my inner pain, no matter how much it hurts.
5. I am going to be the person God created me to be.
6. I am a great person, inside and out. I will receive my healing.

Say these sentences several times a day to yourself. Stand in front of the mirror and talk to yourself. You must be determined to get through this. God will help you. Without Him, your healing would never be. But you must also realize that it will take a great deal of hard work on your part for God to be able to do what He does best. You must bolster your attitude every day. You cannot be halfhearted or you'll never conquer that bear within you. Fight! Read! Pray! Meditate! Put your self-awareness to work!

You have already shown you have some determination just by picking up this book with the intention of helping yourself or your loved one. Below are some additional reinforcers that came out of the hearts of determined people. Read these and apply them to your life. Let these words encourage your spirit today. See *The Angry Heart* by Joseph Santoro for a complete list of inspirational quotes.

"Do not be afraid of going slowly; be afraid of standing still." – Chinese Proverb

"Failing doesn't make you a failure, giving up, accepting your failure, refusing to try again does." – Richard Exley

"When the world says give up, hope whispers, 'Try it one more time.'" – H. Jackson Brown Jr.

"It takes courage to live—courage and strength and hope and humor: and courage and strength and hope and humor have to be and are paid for with pain and work and progress and tears." – Jerome P. Fleishman

"By all means, don't say 'If I can'; say, 'I will.'" – Abraham Lincoln

"Success consists of a series of little daily efforts." – Mamie McCullough

"One of the greatest discoveries a man makes, one of his great surprises, is to find he can do what he was afraid he couldn't do." – Henry Ford

"The best way out of a difficult situation is through it!" – Unknown

I really love these quotes. These are the oil of wisdom you can apply to your rusty joints every day. Looking back through the process of my healing, I had that oil can out quite often, applying a drop wherever and whenever I needed one.

I want you to choose a few quotes from Santoro's book and keep them handy. Post them where you can see them every day; for instance, the two places where you will be every day—the bathroom and the kitchen. I would suggest posting one on the bathroom mirror and one on the fridge. The quotes can be changed as needed.

I have come to realize in my fifty-seven years that we need each other. Sometime or other you will need somebody and/or somebody else will need you! Don't ever look at yourself as a hopeless case. You have value because you were created by God, and He never makes mistakes. He makes His children "perfect," which in the biblical sense means *complete in Him*.

Chapter 5

Repentance

The apostle Paul said in I Corinthians 15:31, "I protest by your rejoicing which I have in Christ Jesus our Lord, I die daily." Larry Webb, pastor of First Apostolic Church of Milton, Florida, said, "God cannot fix what is broken until you are broken over what needs fixing in your life."

Real life requires death. Death involves the experience of suffering. We must have suffering to attain growth. I truly think we get into the habit of rolling through repentance like taking our multivitamin every morning.

What does your repentance and brokenness look like? Write a one-line statement on how you think Jesus views it.

_____

How do you feel when you are done repenting?

_____

In chapter 1, we discussed self-awareness and honesty. When you come to the point of self-awareness and honesty, it is imperative that you move on to repentance. You may be thinking, *Hey, I'm the one that was abused, or hurt, or led down the wrong path! Why should I have to repent and become broken? Haven't I been broken enough? This just doesn't make sense!*

I know exactly what thoughts will go through your mind because that's what I thought. We don't even realize how we have gradually become bitter, rebellious, angry, and far from God as we trudge along with our enormous sack of baggage over our shoulder. After being abused and mistreated, we weave a cocoon around ourselves and over time we emerge as a different person. It's like we're living in a make-believe shell. We are no longer living in honesty, forgiveness, self-awareness, and love—all of it has been stripped away.

> Search me, O God, and know my heart; try me, and know
> my anxieties: and see if there is any wicked way in me,
> and lead me in the way everlasting. (Psalm 139:23–24)

If God were to search your heart, what do you think He would find?

1. _____

2. _____

3. _____

4. _____

I believe we have lived so long in a make-believe world in which we blame everybody else for our shortcomings and failures that we think all of our flaws are the fault of the abuser. If it wasn't for them, we wouldn't have any issues or stumbling blocks to contend with. But the consequence of continuing to live like this is that we are nothing more than a mere puppet! We are hanging by a string. Each time someone jerks our string (offends us), we have no other option but to jump at their command. We have no life of our own. Somebody else owns us!

Dr. Dan B. Allender, in his book *The Wounded Heart*, states, "The process of change begins with honesty, which is a form of repentance. Repentance is an about-face movement from denial and rebellion to truth and surrender—from death to life." When you start on the path of honesty, you are really embarking on the path of repentance. It's impossible to look at everything with honesty and not see the actions and words you have done and said to others, even though your reactions stemmed from the abuse you suffered. If you will be patient and allow someone to help you and work with you, you will be able to handle the reality of your words and actions. It is not pretty. When you become open to God with a broken spirit, you will see the awful truth frame by frame!

This is an extremely crucial time. You will either move forward into repentance or backward into depression and despair. I endured a grueling night of complete despair, and I remember it as if it were yesterday. Until that day I had been unaware of my BPD. Deep down, I had suspected something was wrong, but then as I would cycle and my thinking cleared, I would think, *Oh, I'm fine. Nothing is wrong with me.*

That awful night was pivotal; I had been told that I was in the throes of BPD and had been for many years. Groans issued from the depths of my being. I didn't want to live; I didn't even want to breathe. It felt like I was teetering on the verge of a massive sinkhole. I was about to fall in, never to be seen again. All the words I had said resounded through my mind like a loudspeaker. All of my wrong actions flitted past my mind's eye like reruns. Oh God! Oh God! I can't find the words to describe how I felt about what I had done. I thought I would never be able to fix everything I had done and said. If I had had a gun that night, I think I would have put it to my head and pulled the trigger. I couldn't see anything about me that was good. Brutal honesty and self-revelation had hit in a moment's time, and the enormity of it was so devastating I couldn't see past it. I moaned and groaned for hours, and in between sobs I was praying, "Oh God, help me! Oh God, forgive me!" This was the moment that my eyes were opened to the fact that I could not survive without God.

> *Hiding the past always involves denial; denial of the past is always a denial of God. – Dan B. Allender,* The Wounded Heart

And He said to me, "My grace is sufficient for you, for my strength is made perfect in weakness." (II Corinthians 12:9)

I clung to this verse that night as I sat on the edge of the bed, my soulmate gently wiping the tears from my face. They were streaming down so profusely I couldn't even see. This was probably one of the few times that I felt like I was not going to make it.
I am truly convinced the only thing that saved me that night was repentance—a level of repentance I had never experienced before. I had said and done things under the influence of BPD, and my life

could never be the same again. I had literally destroyed some elements of my family as well as my dear husband's ministry. I couldn't take anything back. What I had done and said was written in indelible ink. I didn't know where to start. What could I say? I thought I'd never be able to face some of those people again.

I heard noises coming from deep within that I didn't even recognize. I mourned the many things we had lost: our house, the church my husband had pastored, the men's ministry he had led for eleven years, and our income. Everything that could be shaken was shaken. I imagined my sweet husband must have felt as Job did when he lost everything. And it was all my fault.

I was shaken to the core. Yes, I could have blamed it all on BPD. I could have said, "Well, it wasn't really me saying and doing all of those things." Although this was true, in part, and the whole world was about to know what I had been struggling with, it was essential that I become broken before God and repent for what had come out of my mouth and my actions. Someone has to take responsibility. Someone has to be willing to stand up and say, "God, I was the one who said those statements and did those things. I repent, God. I prostrate myself before you, my King . . ." And as I sat there repenting, I felt the hand of God reach down and touch me. Somehow, with God's help, I made it through that night.

According to Allender, repentance consists of four components:

1. An internal shift in our perceived source of life
2. The process of deeply acknowledging the supreme call to love
3. A hungry, broken return to God
4. The law of love removes excuses

Repentance oftentimes will begin when you become dissatisfied—when you realize, like the prodigal son, you are sick of eating garbage. At some point you get weary of feeling the way you do, like you are hauling around an entire truckload of garbage. Not only that, but it stinks! Every time you throw the trash over your shoulder and into the truck, you are adding to the stench. You will soon get to the place where no one wants to hang around you. You have become a garbage pile.

The moment we take total responsibility, we have some repenting to do, even for things we had never thought were classified as sinful. Before, you always thought you had a way out. You felt justified in what you said or the action you took. You may have even gone as far as to say, "Yes, I suppose what I did was wrong, but I did that because so and so abused me and that's just the way I am."

According to Allender, repentance flows from the energy of being stunned, silent, and without excuse for the harm you've done to yourself and others, and most of all, for breaking the heart of God. Biblical repentance always leads to life. Unloading all of our garbage at the feet of Jesus cleanses us and sets us free to come alive.

If you are not careful, when you get down on your face to repent before God it can become a pity party. I have been guilty of this many times. I've told God how bad it was for me and I just couldn't help myself. I told Him to change the people who had done me wrong so I could, in turn, do the right thing. I would like to have seen God's face when He heard my prayer. He probably said, "What? You want Me to change the other person so you don't have to change anything you say or do? You don't want to do what's right?"

> "Whatever it takes to draw closer to You, Lord, that's what I'll be willing to do."

When you are in total repentance before God, your shame will dissipate, your heart will soften, and you will be broken. You will know when this occurs. Nobody will have to tell you that you are broken; it will be written all over your face. No more cutting corners or taking illegal shortcuts. You are hanging on a cross, exposed for all to see. There is no more pride. You see your need for your Savior like never before. You know you are nothing without Him—nothing more than a piece of garbage. You need help so desperately that you're willing to do anything He requires.

When we are truly repenting, the person who wronged us comes to mind, and we are able to start putting ourselves in their place. We also can see how we have been abusive in our own behavior due to our past experiences of abuse. We are finally beginning to understand what we have done to others rather than being stuck on what others did to us. We are taking on the mind of Christ. As repentance melts deep down into the crevices of our heart, we see how sinful and ugly our heart is.

What are some of your thoughts so far? Is your heart tugging at you? Take the time to write what you are feeling. There is no right or wrong. Get it out of your head onto paper.

1. _____

2. _____

3. _____

4. _____

5. _____

When someone receives the Holy Spirit there is evidence; they are speaking with other tongues. Even if you cannot hear them speaking in that heavenly language, you can see the glow and smile that comes across their face. Likewise, there must also be evidence of brokenness and change of heart when we have truly repented. It must issue from the depths of our heart and not just be words rattling off our tongue with no reflection, no remorse, no change of heart.

For a victim of abuse, being buried alive is the norm. It makes perfect sense. The problem is they don't realize they are denying their humanness. Their relationships are nothing but robotic motions. There is no depth, passion, or compassion. They are merely existing. It's very difficult for them to open up because this means waking up their emotions and resurrecting from the grave.

An abuse victim resists this resurrection because it puts them at risk for being hurt all over again. Emerging from the grave means they must start trusting again, and that is a very hard thing for an abused man or woman to do. Not only that, when they come alive, their sense of feeling is restored. This means they will experience not only the pain of the abuse, but the pain of what was lost or what could have been.

However, there is an upside: they are also opening up to the truth, and the truth will set them free! It is truly a freedom they have never experienced or felt in a very long time. They make a complete turnaround, and are now able to let God back into their life so He can heal them.

This is one of the beauties of repentance. It puts a person on the right road to wholeness, completeness, truth, and healing. It puts them in a position to take responsibility for their actions. It puts them in a whole new frame of mind—the mind of Christ!

> For who hath known the mind of the Lord, that he may instruct him? But we have the mind of Christ. . . . Let this mind be in you, which was also in Christ Jesus. (I Corinthians 2:16; Philippians 2:5)

When we repent and make a complete turnaround, we are trading fantasy for truth, emptiness for wholeness. We are trading a mixed-up mind for "the mind of Christ." Repentance allows us to open up to new relationships—not necessarily with new people, but better and healthier relationships with the people we love.

Repentance is never a one-time deal; it becomes a lifestyle. We learn how to fully die daily. We can look honestly at ourselves every day and allow God to talk to us, to let us know where we messed up.

A final word on repentance: you only need to repent of something once, not multiple times. When you continue to repent of the same wrong over and over, it leads to depression. Many times people feel so bad about what they have done or said that they think repenting of it only one time is not sufficient. I would like to tell you God only wants to hear about it once, and then He chooses not to remember it anymore. When you constantly bring it back up, God doesn't know what you are talking about. It's done, forgiven, and forgotten.

As we close this chapter, I want you to take some time to think about repentance. Think about how you changed after your abuse or emotional circumstances. Evaluate your communication with people. Think of the sin in your life and what you need to repent of. Open up to your Savior who is mighty to forgive. God in His great mercy sees where you are. He knows you have been emotionally or physically abused. God knows how hard it is for you to open up to truth, repentance, and love. But you can do it.

Chapter 6

Forgiveness

Forgive us our debts, as we forgive our debtors. . . . For if ye forgive men their trespasses, your heavenly Father will also forgive you: but if ye forgive not men their trespasses, neither will your Father forgive your trespasses. (Matthew 6:12, 14–15, KJV)

The need for forgiveness is serious because God said if we don't forgive, *He will not forgive us*. For this reason alone we should be obedient to God's Word. Yet to some, *forgiveness* is a dreaded word; others don't take it seriously or flatly refuse to even try.

According to Paul J. Meyer, forgiveness is the ultimate miracle. "Forgiveness has an uncanny way of bringing incredible good out of incredibly bad situations." Have you ever seen a situation where it looked like there was no hope? I have, and I have witnessed it firsthand in my own life. There is nothing like forgiving someone and letting go of the anger and bitterness. You feel as though your painful shackles have suddenly loosened and fallen off.

As you think about forgiveness, does a particular person or even several people come to mind that you need to forgive but have not done so for one reason or another? Write their names. If you aren't sure whether or not you have forgiven someone, write that also. Take it from me: if you don't know if you have forgiven, then you haven't.

1. _____

2. _____

3. _____

4. _____

5. _____

As I climbed into the car and pulled the door shut on that rainy day, I knew God was with me. I needed Him desperately. "God, please go before me and help me to say the right words. Let me go in there with a bushel of mercy and grace, because I have an abundance of mercy and grace You have given to me. If You go with me, I can walk in there and be like You." As I walked into the building where I was to meet my abuser face to face, I wanted to forgive as Joseph forgave. One of my favorite stories on forgiveness is the story of Joseph (Genesis 38–45). I get teary-eyed every time I read it. It moves my spirit and convicts my soul.

It is hard to imagine what it would be like if I were in Joseph's place and knew my brothers hated me. How much hatred would it take for them to want to murder their youngest brother? How could they throw him into a pit and ignore his cries for help? How could they sell him into slavery and not care where he would end up? They compounded their betrayal when they slaughtered a goat, dipped Joseph's torn coat into the blood, and took it home to their father. Feigning sadness, they told their father Joseph had been killed by a wild animal and dragged somewhere into the desert. They had searched but never found him. How could they tell such a cruel lie and not even care about their father's broken heart?

Joseph's suffering did not end in the pit; it had just begun. On the journey to Egypt, shackles bloodied his ankles as he was dragged over the rough caravan route. At night they put him in irons (Psalm 105:17–18). Upon arrival in Egypt, his captors sold him as a slave. He served his master faithfully, only to be falsely accused and thrown into prison where he was locked up several more years. Yet when Joseph came face to face with his brothers many years later, he felt compassion for them and forgave them.

As I was about to talk face to face with the person who had sexually abused me and done so much harm in my life, I wanted to forgive as Joseph forgave his brothers. In his book, *Total Forgiveness*, R. T. Kendall maintains there are seven steps in the process of forgiveness. I have taken these seven steps and applied them to my own life; as you read, I would like you to begin applying them to your own life as well.

1. Don't tell anyone what your offender did to you or said about you. At the climax of the story, Joseph waited until everyone had left the room before he revealed his true identity to his brothers.

> Then Joseph could not restrain himself before all those who stood by him, and he cried out, "Make everyone go out from me!" So no one stood with him while Joseph made himself known to his brothers. (Genesis 45:1)

An overwhelming compassion must have swept over Joseph at this moment. He must have pondered long and hard about how to confront his brothers, because he dismissed all the members of the court. He knew if the Egyptians found out what his brothers had done to him, they would punish them. He couldn't allow that; he wanted his entire family to be with him. He assured them, "No one will know. I will take care of you."

This is how God forgives us. Our sins are never brought up again or repeated to anybody else. "As far as the east is from the west, so far has He removed our transgressions from us. . . . I, even I, am He who blots out your transgressions for My own sake; and I will not remember your sins" (Psalm 103:12; Isaiah 43:25). Notice that God said He forgives "for His own sake." In effect, this is what happens when you forgive: you extend forgiveness to others so you can receive God's forgiveness.

Like Joseph, I did not want anybody else witnessing or knowing what I was doing when I forgave the one who had offended me. It was all done in private. It was just us and God. That's all that needed to be there.

2. Do not intimidate or accuse your offender. Joseph did not want his brothers to be afraid of retribution. He revealed who he was with tears streaming down his face. He wept so loudly that the Egyptians heard him from another room (Genesis 45:2). If we have not truly forgiven, we will get pleasure in seeing our offender quaking in his boots when he sees us coming. We might say to ourselves, "Good! He should be afraid!" We feel his fear is part of the punishment he deserves. But forgiveness extends a hand and says, "Come close to me; do not be afraid."

There is no fear in love; but perfect love casts out fear, because fear involves torment. But he who fears has not been made perfect in love. (I John 4:18)

As I was talking with my offender, I assured him he needn't say anything. I didn't want him to be apprehensive or groping for words to say. I stood close with compassion and gentleness.

3. Do try to get them to forgive themselves and not feel guilty. We are tempted to go into great detail so they will remember every action and emotion, but we have a big problem if we want to send people on a guilt trip. Do you know people like this? When they walk away, it's like they dumped a bucket of ice water on you. It feels terrible! But Joseph even went so far as to say, "It was God who sent me here, not you." (See Genesis 45:5.)

When we refuse to lower the boom on someone, it makes it so much easier for them to see what they have done and paves the way for them to deal with it. This makes it easier for them to offer you an apology, repent, and give their sin to God. It helps them to walk forward, leave everything behind, and build on their future with confidence and security.

4. Do allow them to save face. Allowing our offender to save face is carrying the principle of true forgiveness a step further. Saving face means salvaging one's dignity and self-esteem. It is the refusal to make the other person feel guilty. It is hiding a person's error so they won't be embarrassed in front of others. You will make a friend for life by letting them save face.

This is exactly what God does for us. He lets us save face by causing our past, no matter how bad, to work out for our good. When we can put ourselves in the offender's place, it's easy to let them save face. If we were in their shoes, we too would want to save face. When we see ourselves as we really are, we will have to admit that we are just as capable of committing the same sin as anyone else.

That day I truly wanted to allow my offender to save face. It was quite an embarrassing sin for him after all. We both knew what had occurred. It wasn't about getting every detail right and naming everything for what it was. This saved him much embarrassment, emotion, guilt, and shame. When you allow your offender to save face, all parties can walk away contented, at peace, and able to move on.

5. Do protect your offender from his greatest fear. Can you imagine how Joseph's brothers felt after the truth had been revealed? The account in Genesis 42 tells us they had become agitated and apprehensive when Joseph had earlier accused them of being spies. They spoke among themselves, unaware that Joseph could understand every word: "We are truly guilty concerning our brother, for we saw the anguish of his soul when he pleaded with us, and we would not hear; therefore this distress has come upon us" (v. 21). So when Joseph finally revealed his true identity, his brothers' fears probably increased exponentially. They feared the worst. What kind of trouble would their offense bring down upon their heads in this strange land? They were at Joseph's mercy; he could have them punished any way he wished. Barring that, would Joseph make them go back home and tell their aging father the gross sins they had committed?

But sin that is under the blood doesn't need to be told to anybody except God. For instance, my father passed away before I wrote my first book, *Buried Alive.* Even though my mother has read my book, she doesn't know who my abuser was and she will never know. It's under the blood and forgiven forever.

Joseph did not order his brothers to return home and admit their sin to Jacob. Instead, he told them to tell their father he was alive and wanted to take care of his family during the rest of the famine.

> Hurry and go up to my father, and say to him, "Thus says your son Joseph: 'God has made me lord of all Egypt; come down to me, do not tarry. You shall dwell in the land of Goshen, and you shall be near to me, you and your children, your flocks and your herds, and all that you have. There I will provide for you, lest you and your household, and all that you have, come to poverty; for there are still five years of famine.'" And behold, your eyes and the eyes of my brother Benjamin see that it is my mouth that speaks to you. So you shall tell my father of all my glory in Egypt, and of all that you have seen;

and you shall hurry and bring my father down here. (Genesis 45:9–13)

Should Joseph's brothers have been forced to confess to their father their sins against Joseph? No, this information would have burdened their father with an impossible load of bitterness against his other sons. It would have been detrimental to the mental and physical health of a man of his advanced years. Joseph was very wise and fair.

We must protect our offender by letting it be known only to the people who must know, such as our counselor or accountability partner. The only exception to this is a case that involves criminal action.

6. Do treat forgiveness as a lifelong commitment. Don't forgive one day, then return to pick up the offense the next day. After Jacob had passed away, Joseph's brothers were once again afraid of Joseph. They were terrified that the brother whom they had victimized had been biding his time until after their father's death to wreak vengeance on them for their sin.

> When Joseph's brethren saw that their father was dead, they said, "Perhaps Joseph will hate us, and may actually repay us for all the evil which we did to him. (Genesis 50:15)

Joseph wept when he saw that his brothers doubted him.

> Joseph said to them, "Do not be afraid, for am I in the place of God? But as for you, you meant evil against me, but God meant it for good, in order to bring it about as it is this day, to save many people alive. Now therefore, do not be afraid: I will provide for you and your little ones." And he comforted them and spoke kindly to them. (Genesis 50:19–21)

The secret of his brothers' betrayal that Joseph had kept for more than seventeen years still held good. He continued to keep that secret until his dying day. We must never reveal an abuse so that our offender can live free from fear. True forgiveness is a lifelong commitment. I told my offender the wrongdoing was under the blood. The offense was gone, washed away like water under the bridge.

God never brings our sins back to haunt us. Satan may try to bring them back; we may try to bring them back; but God will not. There is never any doubt or fear after God has forgiven us.

7. Do pray for your offender to be blessed. True forgiveness includes a final step: you must pray for your offender to be blessed. Think about the magnitude of this. You are praying, "God, bless my offender. Show him or her mercy and grace. I give them to You, God!" When you pray for your offender this way, it's hard to get upset with them or go back on your pledge of forgiveness. It's difficult to feel ill will toward them. And it's a lot harder to think about what they did to you; instead, you will be thinking about how God will bless them. If we have really forgiven we want them to prosper. We want God to show them mercy and grace. We don't want the offense to cause them to fail. I will go a step further: I think it's good to pray for the people who dislike us. This keeps our hearts right and our spirits pure. This is how we should pray:

> Our Father which art in heaven, Hallowed be thy name. Thy kingdom come. Thy will be done in earth, as it is in heaven. Give us this day our daily bread. And forgive us our debts, as we forgive our debtors. And lead us not into temptation, but deliver us from evil: for thine is the kingdom, and the power, and the glory, for ever. Amen. (Matthew 6:9–13, KJV)

This prayer shows that you need forgiveness as much as you need daily bread. You cannot allow bitterness and unforgiveness to remain in your heart and expect to live a healthy, happy life full of great relationships. It would be like a ship trying to make headway in the ocean with its anchor dragging in the mud at the bottom. It would be impossible to live a productive life. They say that bitterness kills the container it's in. You may deny you are bitter, but self-deception is easy. And it doesn't take long for bitterness to set in and take up residence.

Are you thinking about the list of people you named at the beginning of this chapter? Is your heart beginning to hurt a little? Are there, in fact, more people you need to forgive? God is tugging at your heartstrings, prompting you to do the right thing. Write your thoughts in the space provided below.

1. _____

2. _____

3. _____

4. _____

5. _____

6. _____

I want to share a story with you about forgiveness. In 2012, Vicki Richardson, my daughter, Kaitlin, and I traveled to Liberia, Africa, to speak at a Ladies Conference. It was a trip I will never forget, and I'd love to return someday. The Albert Stewarts were still missionaries in Liberia at that time. They cooked every meal for us as there wasn't anywhere else where the food was safe for us to eat.

The conference went well, and we enjoyed a great move of God in the services. When it was time to leave, we packed up and went to the airport, where we hit a snag. Hurricane Sandy had torn through New York City, flooding the underground subway system, causing fires that destroyed numerous homes and businesses, and shutting down the New York Stock Exchange for two consecutive days. Since New York City was our layover destination, we were sent back home with the Stewarts.

I wouldn't give anything for those two extra days with the Stewarts. They told us stories about the Liberian Civil War they had gone through. Following is an excerpt from an article in the July-August 1991 *Global Witness* that gives a brief description of the war-torn conditions:

> There was no food and people were without money. The streets were filled with bodies of the dead or dying as a result of starvation. Testimonies from our believers there

related of children dying because of the lack of food or money. If Compassion Services International had not sent the food and clothing, and Brother [Albert] Stewart had not been here we were all going to die. We were dying on our feet. Thank you, thank you for coming to our rescue. Please continue to remember us in Liberia.

Brother Stewart told of a lady who came to him with a question on forgiveness. During the Civil War her husband had been decapitated by the leader of a tribe. Not only that, but they had paraded through the town with her husband's head impaled on a stick for everyone to see. The final irony was that the man who did this heinous act later came into the church and received the Holy Spirit, and he was attending the same church this lady attended. She asked, "Brother Stewart, do I have to forgive him after what he did to my husband?" Brother Stewart had no choice but to give her a biblical answer: "Yes, dear lady, you must. You see, the Bible doesn't give us a list of offenses that are just too bad to forgive."

If you think someone has done something too bad for you to forgive, think back to this story. There are many more where this came from. People have gone through hell and back again and still had the capacity to forgive. So did Jesus! Paul J. Meyer concludes, "Forgiveness runs deeper than unforgiveness." There is nothing too deep or too hurtful that cannot be forgiven.

Forgiveness and your self-image hang together. You cannot separate the two. You cannot truly feel good about yourself while harboring unforgiveness in your heart. But when you forgive, you will have peace and joy. You will know that no matter what happens you followed through with what the Bible instructed you to do. You can walk away blameless.

I do not have the words to describe how wonderful I felt after forgiving my offender. That hurdle made it easier for me to forgive several other people in my life. You see, many hurts can accumulate over a lifetime. Many offenses happen unintentionally, but they still affect you and you must forgive. And forgiveness flows into place after repentance.

I have heard some dear people say how hard it is to forgive. But after my experience, I have to say when you are truly repentant and broken and see your faults under a spotlight, it is easy to stand at the foot of the cross, look the offender in the eyes, and say with sincerity, "I forgive you." We are all capable of sin, given the right place and time and attitude. But when you see that you are no better than they, you can forgive.

What would our fate be if God forgave everyone in the same manner that we forgive? What would happen if we stood before God and told Him what we did, and He stood there trying to decide whether or not He was willing to forgive us? God's forgiveness doesn't work that way. His love is unconditional, and His forgiveness is full of love! I pray that on the day God chooses to take me home to be with Him, I will be able to go peacefully, knowing I have no one left to forgive. Ever since my pivotal experience of total repentance, I have lived a life of total forgiveness. It is sad to hear of someone who, on their death bed, has to make last-minute calls to forgive someone.

What will it be like for you? Will you choose to forgive and be set free, or are you going to stay chained to the anvil and planning revenge?

If you followed the principles of repentance in the previous chapter, this chapter on forgiveness will not be a big issue or a hard thing to do. If it has been hard for you, I urge you to go back to repentance and brokenness and let God talk to your heart and release you from the shackles. My friend, you can forgive, and doing so will free both you and your offenders. Remember you can do all things through Christ who strengthens you!

Let me encourage you today. *Forgive*! It will set you free!

Chapter 7

Restitution: Put to Rest

When was the last time you heard someone bring up the subject of restitution? Repentance, yes. Forgiveness, yes. But a discussion about restitution? That one draws a blank.

Have you ever done someone wrong and maybe even apologized for it, but never made it right? Can you think of someone off the top of your head that you need to make restitution to right now? Write their name(s) on the lines below.

1. _____

2. _____

3. _____

What do you need to do to bring restitution to them? To bring peace to their spirit? Write it down below. If you don't know the answer, ask them what you need to do.

1. _____

2. _____

3. _____

As I began writing this chapter, I noticed something I had not noticed before: the first four letters of the word *restitution* spell "rest." When you do what you can to bring restitution to somebody you have wronged, the relationship is restored. Trouble and unrest are no longer on the books. The outstanding debit in the ledger is cancelled out. Forgiving someone without making restitution leaves something undone. It's like washing dishes but never putting them away. It's like attending school but dropping out in the eleventh grade.

Unrecompensed situations must be put to rest. There must be an act of taking back what you said not only to the one you hurt but also to all the people you have told about the situation and let them believe what they will.

Included in the restitution (apology) must be an admission of wrongdoing. Being willing to say "I was wrong" indicates two things: (1) you admit to yourself that you were wrong, and (2) you acknowledge to them that you were wrong. Saying you're sorry without admitting you were wrong leaves the act unfinished and incomplete. Anyone can simply say they're sorry and leave it at that. It means that in their mind and spirit they are still holding on to their side, their conclusion, and their belief that they really did no wrong. Just saying you're sorry makes a sorry apology.

How would you feel if you found out someone was spreading false rumors about you to all their friends? When you confront them about it, they say, "Oh, I'm sorry." What about all the people they have gone to with the tale? What if those people still believe those untrue things about you? Is saying "I'm sorry" going to put the matter to rest? Is an apology like that going to make you feel as if the record is erased, your mind is at ease, and you can go on? Or are you going to constantly wonder who is believing what about you? What is everyone thinking when you walk into a room?

> *Restitution means recompense for injury or loss; compensation, reparation,*

I can probably count on one hand the times I've heard someone mention restitution or preach about it. Anytime someone said they had to "make things right" with someone, they were usually referring to asking for forgiveness, not making restitution.

We are pretty good about replacing something we borrowed that broke when it was in our care. If our children are out playing ball in the yard and their fly ball crashes through a neighbor's window, we step up and pay for the replacement cost. This is easy to do because it doesn't involve taking back our words. It doesn't involve brokenness. Thus, making restitution for tangible things isn't hard; recompensing wrongs for intangible things is.

Think of someone who needs to make restitution for something they did to you, but they have not. Write down what it is.

1. _____

2. _____

3. _____

4. _____

How is this lack of restitution affecting your life? Has it kept you off balance?

1. _____

2. _____

Dwight L. Moody declared, "If we have done wrong to anyone, we should never ask God to forgive us until we are willing to make restitution." I would wonder how sincere the apology was if there was no restitution made—because, according to the Bible, restitution is the action that should naturally follow forgiveness. When we repent of our sins, our repentance is not complete until we root out everything associated with that sin. We do what we need to do in order to show God we really mean it. "God, I am sorry for what I did. I will do whatever it takes to change, to show You I am making a change." For instance, let's say we have slacked off in our prayer time or have been skipping days of prayer. We tell God how sorry we are and that we intend to do better. The only way God is going to see we are changing and we really mean business is to start praying every day and extend our prayer time. Why don't we do this with each other? If you have no intention of making restitution, your apology is just wasted words.

As I sat on the bedside that night, God came into the room and lifted the blinders off my eyes so I could see the brutal reality of my wrongs. I was crying so hard I felt almost delirious. For the first time, I saw how deadly my words and actions were. "Oh my God! Please come into this room and help me! I don't know if I can ever show my face again!" If I ever had a suicidal moment, that was it! If the earth would have opened up and swallowed me, I would have been grateful.

I felt like a total failure. How could I have brought so much damage to my own life and the lives of others? The words I would have to eat were pure poison! It would take some time to conquer these feelings and make restitution to everyone. But I knew it had to be done.

I couldn't muster up the right words to say, but God heard my groaning and knew what it meant. There weren't any words that were sufficient enough to repent of what I had done. Borderline Personality Disorder had taken its toll on me. It had led me down a road I would never have chosen had I been free of the disorder.

When BPD takes over, your thoughts and feelings seem so real. You think you know the truth, but in reality your thinking is terribly skewed. For example, if you feel no one loves you, you will produce words and actions that express that feeling. But if your feelings exist only in your mind and not in reality, any words or actions that follow are just as skewed as your thinking. It is an unending cycle of self-deception and despair.

Even though I probably would not have walked the road I did had it not been for BPD, I still had done a lot of wrong and hurt many people along the way. This realization tore through my mind and emotions like a cyclone. It finally passed, leaving destruction in its wake. Groping my way through the wreckage, I knew there was a long road ahead to right all the wrongs. It was going to take some time and some healing. For me restitution was widespread. It was overwhelming. I thought, *Where do I even begin?* I saw how many people I had affected and the losses all of us had suffered. *Oh my Lord!* I knew the damage was so great that no amount of restitution would salvage it all. Some things were lost forever. It had affected my entire family, a great deal of friends, and my husband's ministry as well as my own. Among the things that were lost forever were our home, the church my husband pastored, the men's ministry he had led, and our reputation with the presbyter of our section. My words and actions had thrown all those things out the window.

Making restitution of this magnitude must be done very carefully. Timing is crucial, along with what is said and how it's done. This is where your support team is of great value. Some restitutions must be done through your pastor and counselor. It is a process that takes reflection, good judgment, and proper timing.

My process of restitution had to be thought out strategically. My heart faltered when I thought about going back to people and explaining about the disorder that had triggered my words and actions. It would be tough, but nonetheless, it had to be done. I will say the first time was the hardest, but one by one, as I went to people, I realized that making restitution brought rest and healing to all involved, including me.

I couldn't bear the thought of how I sat before a district board and defamed their reputations. How could I fix that? With the help of my dear pastor and counselor, I developed a letter in my own words that I could send each member of the board. I also composed a letter to send to any friend or acquaintance to whom I had said anything or even hinted anything. I wanted to be sure everything was made right and nothing was left undone.

Furthermore, I had to reach a certain point in my healing process before sending out these letters because I would eventually come face to face with all these people. What would they think about me? Would they still love me? Would they ever be able to trust me again? Would my words mean nothing to them? With all of these thoughts running through my head, I had to be healed enough to survive this without a relapse of BPD or a trigger that would send me over the edge. My pastor helped me to make sure everyone in the wider context of my life received a letter. In addition, every saint in the church where we had pastored for twenty years also needed a letter. Of course, upon leaving the church and all the turmoil that ensued, some sheep had scattered to other places. We had to track those down. So you can see why I used the adjective "widespread" restitution. It took tremendous effort.

> Eventually I would come face to face with all these people. What would they think about me? Would they still love me? Would they ever be able to trust me again?

After the letters were sent out, I then had to prepare myself for the reactions I would receive from all of these people. I will say, for the most part their words were kind, understanding, and encouraging. Unfortunately, there were a few who rejected my overture, choosing to believe things the way they saw it. It saddened me. You see, when people don't accept restitution, they are rejecting the good and true, and believing the worst. Their pride won't let them accept or admit that the things they have believed for so long aren't true. They want to believe their assumptions are correct.

Here are a few Scripture verses that helped me a great deal during this time.

> I can do all things through Christ who strengthens me. (Philippians 4:13)

> For God has not given us a spirit of fear, but of power and of love and of a sound mind. (II Timothy 1:7)

> Let us therefore come boldly to the throne of grace that we may obtain mercy and find grace to help in time of need. (Hebrews 4:16).

I want to assure you that God is your ever-present help in time of trouble. Even though you mess up or fail, if you are trying to make things right at all cost, God is on your side. He has more grace and mercy than you can comprehend. He has a vast storehouse, and whatever you need, He will never run out of it!

Take a good look at your past. If you were suffering from an emotional disorder, addiction, or any other affliction, were your words and actions Christlike? It's easy to find fault with our offender and point fingers, but we should be courageous enough to take a look at ourselves. What do we need to do? Yes, our behavior stemmed from our abuse and subsequent disorder/addiction, but at some point we must take responsibility and make right all of our wrongs. Taking responsibility means we must make a change, and that is very hard to do for most because we want everybody else to change, not us.

Think deeply about this and write down some wrongs you have done. Maybe you have apologized for them but have not taken responsibility and therefore have not made restitution.

1. _____

2. _____

3. _____

4. _____

5. _____

6. _____

Look over what you have written and list the restitution you need to
do to put everything to rest.

1. _____

2. _____

3. _____

4. _____

5. _____

6. _____

Is someone hurting because you have not taken the time and
effort to make restitution? Are you willing to make the sacrifice?
When you do, it will bring freedom and rest to your spirit and theirs.
Do you want to be blameless? When a person is blameless, there are
no grounds—or basis or reason—for accusation because he has made
every effort to correct the wrong and reconcile the relationship in
truth. In this sense, a blameless person is irreproachable. He takes the
initiative to be transparent with everyone. He can be held up to the
light of truth and found to be completely clear because he has
confessed it all. Just because he is blameless does not mean he has
never made a mistake; but as far as he is able, physically, materially,
and spiritually, he has done everything within his power to
acknowledge where he was wrong, to correct it where possible, and to
make any appropriate restitution to restore fellowship. After you have
done all you can do in your circle of responsibility, the only thing left
is to stand still and leave the results of your efforts with God.

God is serious about restitution. He wrote it into the Law in
Exodus 22, where He gave eight scenarios that characterize offenses
that would require restitution. In the New Testament, Jesus simplified
the idea of restitution (reconciliation) in the Sermon on the Mount.

Therefore if you bring your gift to the altar, and there remember that your brother has something against you, leave your gift there before the altar, and go your way. First be reconciled to your brother and then come and offer your gift. (Matthew 5:23–24)

God does not want to hear your prayer until you are reconciled to your brother! That sounds serious to me. That tells me you cannot walk in the light or have the mind of Christ when you have not offered restitution to restore relationship.

Remember that some restitution will be a complex process and will require patience and time. It might even extend over the course of several years, depending on how complicated the situation is. For others it might be resolved with a short phone call.

I believe you will make the right decision. You can do it! You can be blameless before God!

Chapter 8

Your Prayer Life

Prayer, or communicating with God, is one of the most important things we can do. Prayer is the backbone of everything. Without prayer there is nothing. I would say just about everybody who struggles with issues in their life has an insufficient prayer life. Everything we fight, whether in the body or the spirit, affects our relationship with God.

Inconsistency is a hallmark symptom of Borderline Personality Disorder, and it has been a battle for me as long as I can remember. For a Borderline, consistency is impossible because everything is weighed according to feelings—and feelings can fluctuate and even lie. They can blow things up way out of proportion. They can turn on a dime. So every morning when a Borderline wakes up and asks, "Do I feel like praying today or not?" the decision is made on feelings and moods rather than fact and consistency.

When every decision is made on emotion, life is like a rollercoaster. Patterns are never established; decisions are made on a whim. This creates anxiety and depression in your life because you are always second-guessing yourself. You have nothing to go on but emotion. Most people without BPD can make decisions based on facts. They have a firmer foundation in reality and can look back and say, "Yes, I made the right decision." I'm not saying emotion will not factor in at all—emotion will weigh in on either side of a scale to a certain extent—but decisions that are based primarily on the facts surrounding the circumstances or situation will generally lead to a sounder, more stable, more productive outcome.

> *But we will give ourselves continually to prayer and to the ministry of the word. (Acts 6:4)*

In the space provided, write down your patterns of prayer. Do you pray only when you need something or when trouble comes your way? Do you pray only when someone is demanding more out of you regarding time spent in conversation with God?

1. _____

2. _____

3. _____

4. _____

5. _____

6. _____

It is very important to have someone who will hold you accountable to begin each day with prayer and guidance from God; it might be the only thing that saves you. Is there someone you could partner with and pray together every day? If not in person, maybe over the phone. Think about this and write down a few people who could be a help to you.

1. _____

2. _____

3. _____

There are several other reasons besides BPD why people often have a hard time with prayer. For example, people often compare their heavenly Father to their earthly father. You may not even be aware that you have put up a wall between you and God because of it. If your father was physically abusive, you may feel as though God is holding a baseball bat over your head and the first mistake you make—*bam!* In order to avoid that, you say, "I won't even go there" and not pray at all. If you do this, you will suffer tremendously, because without a prayer life I guarantee you will not make it. Prayerlessness sets you up for failure.

Some have a father who is distant. I loved my father very much but he grew up in the old school. The way he showed his love for his family was by providing for us financially. At one point he was working at two or three jobs with the result that he was absent most of the time. In his early forties Dad started a successful business, which took up a great deal more of his time. Dad never learned how to show affection; his parents were all work and no play. That's all he knew. So although none of this was intentional, it still affected the entire family. I grew up thinking God was cold, uncaring, and so far away He could never be a close friend. I had to learn that God was "as close as the mention of His name."

Some people don't know their father because they've never met him. I once knew a man I'll call Ted. When he was a young boy, his father refused to have anything to do with him and abandoned Ted and his mother. Many years later Ted was walking down the main street of the little town where they lived, when all of a sudden he spotted his father. In a burst of emotion, Ted called out to him, but the old man turned on his heel and walked the other way as if he didn't even know or want to know his son. Ted had a hard time believing that his heavenly Father loved him and claimed him as His own. There are many more sad stories that people deal with every day.

Did you have a father who demanded perfection? They say that one of the hardest things for a child to live with is a critical parent. Some people give up because no matter what they do, they can't please their parent. Some people would rather not try at all than to fumble the ball and then suffer the criticism. They can't help but transfer these feelings to God, thinking He will not accept anything from them unless it's absolutely perfect.

Write down what kind of father you had. Be honest.

_____

After writing what kind of father you had or have, what behaviors have you taken on because of it?

1. _____

2. _____

3. _____

What you wrote in the exercise above in no way indicates that you don't love or care for your father. This is just taking an honest look at how your father's behavior has affected your relationship and prayer life with God.

Your heavenly Father worked nine months creating you in your mother's womb. His thoughts toward you, His creation, are infinitely loving and nurturing.

> I will praise thee; for I am fearfully and wonderfully made: marvellous are thy works; and that my soul knoweth right well. My substance was not hid from thee, when I was made in secret, and curiously wrought in the lowest parts of the earth. Thine eyes did see my substance, yet being unperfect; and in thy book all my members were written, which in continuance were fashioned, when as yet there was none of them. How precious also are thy thoughts unto me, O God! how great is the sum of them! If I should count them, they are more in number than the sand: when I awake, I am still with thee. (Psalm 139:14–18, KJV)

This is what our heavenly Father thinks about us. This is our God whom we are praying to, with whom we are striving to have an intimate relationship. I want to assure you that God loves you more than you can ever know. You can believe this with your whole heart, soul, and mind. He cares about every little detail of your life. When you begin to understand that God's love for you is beyond your wildest dreams, you will then be able to grow in your prayer life and your relationship with your Creator.

According to Brady Boyd in *Speak Life,* the most common question he is asked as a pastor is, "Does God really speak to me?" I too am often asked the same question. I think sometimes you try too hard to hear God's voice. You must understand that God doesn't have only one avenue through which He speaks to you. He uses various ways to get your attention. He will speak to you in prayer—you just have to be patient enough to wait and listen. He will speak to you through your thoughts, sometimes leaving a strong impression. One gauge I use to know if it is God communicating with me is when something comes to me over and over again and does not seem to go away.

I once had a divine appointment through a strong impression. I had prayed that morning and was starting to run errands for the day. As I was heading for the grocery store, God impressed me to go to Hobby Lobby. I let the thought roll carelessly through my mind like a bowling ball that misses all ten pins. I thought, *Really God?* As I continued through the list of errands, God kept telling me: *Hobby Lobby, Hobby Lobby, Hobby Lobby*. I finally said, "Okay, okay, God! Hobby Lobby it is." I pulled into the parking lot wondering what in the world God wanted me to do at Hobby Lobby. As I walked into the store, God said, "Go straight back." I walked all the way to the sewing department at the back of the store and saw a lady, a Hobby Lobby employee, standing there straightening out spools of thread. God said, "There she is."

I just stood there asking God, "What do you want me to say?" God said, "Just start talking to her and I will give you the words to say." I thought, *Oh great.* But I figured I had come this far and, after all, I wanted to be obedient to God. So I walked up to the lady and said, "I just want you to know that God loves you and really cares about what you're going through—because He sent me here to tell you."

Immediately her eyes filled and she said, "I can't believe it! You've given me such hope to know that God really does love me!" As we stood talking, my heart warmed toward her. I was so thankful I was obedient that day and followed the Lord's instructions.

Has there been a time when God spoke to you? Has He encouraged you and lifted you up? Has He given you a word or insight into your future? Write down your experience(s) on the lines below. Take your time and think about it.

1. _____

2. _____

3. _____

4. _____

I believe a lot of people get discouraged with their prayer time because they think they don't hear from God. One thing that has helped me in prayer is knowing I have to tarry. There have been times when I have prayed about something and I didn't receive an answer during prayer time. But as someone was talking to me, something would shift in my spirit, or I would read something, or out of nowhere something would come to my mind. When things like this happen, make note of it. Many times it is God speaking to you.

Many people have a hard time knowing what to say in prayer. I think we forget God was once in human flesh walking and living on the earth. He has experienced every human feeling and thought the same kind of thoughts. I want to assure you that God is your friend. You can talk to Him just as you would talk to your closest friend.

Some things need to be prayed every day.

1. *Repent.* I must keep my heart clean and empty of any sin in order to grow. If and when I detect anything I need to forgive, I start that moment, not three days later. When I feel a hurt deep down in my heart after something was said or done to me, I start not only forgiving that person but also praying God's mercy and blessing over them. This keeps my heart clean. I don't want anything to stay there long enough to build a nest in my heart, because it would block the channel of communication with Him just as a bird's nest can block a chimney.

2. *Plead the blood.* I plead the blood over my mind, that God will cover my mind with protection. Everything starts in the mind and imagination, and that's where the battles are fought. If I can keep my mind clear of anything that opposes God or His will for me, I will win the battle.

3. *Ask God to guide your steps.* Every day I ask God to lead me. He has a plan for every day. There are no wasted days in God's kingdom, so I try to make every day count.

4. *Ask for help with the tasks He has assigned.* I ask God to help me in whatever project I'm involved with at the time. I have been writing books for a while now, so my constant prayer is that God will help me to write the words that will touch hearts and minister to people. I don't want to just churn out another book; I want God's

anointing and blessing upon what I write so it will touch the hearts of people who are hurting. I must be about my Father's business each day, reaching for people and knowing He will be right there reaching with me.

5. Tell God you can't live without Him. I let God know I cannot make it through a day without Him. I've come to realize that I have to have Him by my side. This admission does not make me weak; it makes a statement that I know who my God is and how powerful He is. I have learned that without God I am nothing. My own goodness is like a pile of filthy rags. Only God can clean me up and make me look good. God loves it when I depend on Him. I don't want to live one day without Him.

6. Thank God for healing. I thank God for the healing He has done in my life. Praise God! I will always be thankful for His healing power. I thank Him for saving me, for dying on the cross for my sins. If it hadn't been for Jesus, where would I be? I praise Him for the awesome God that He is. He is my Deliverer. He is my Healer. He is my ever-present help in the time of need.

> For we are His workmanship, created in Christ Jesus for good works, which God prepared beforehand that we should walk in them. (Ephesians 2:10)

7. Ask God for advice. God is the One who formed me, both naturally and spiritually. I am His workmanship, which means He knows everything about me. We as parents love it when our children come to us and ask, "Mom/Dad, can you tell me how I should do this? How does it work?" It gives us a good feeling inside because our children love and respect us enough to want our opinion and guidance. God is our heavenly Father, and it gives Him great pleasure when we say, "God, I need some help with this. I have no clue how to fix this or what to say!" I'm sure God's response is, "I'm glad you asked!"

Have you ever had a friend, let's say a guy named Arlo, who would take zero advice from you or anybody else? What did you think about him? Was he fun to be around? Were you able to have a satisfying relationship with him? Probably not. You probably don't feel one ounce of closeness or intimacy with Arlo. He doesn't trust you enough to ask for your opinion or advice about anything. Is this the way the Lord feels when we act like we don't need Him? There is no true relationship, no closeness. This must make God sad in that He knows everything about us and could help us live a much fuller, more exciting life.

8. Be satisfied with the day He has made. I must decide during my prayer time that "this is the day which the LORD hath made; [I] will rejoice and be glad in it" (Psalm 118:24, KJV). I must purpose in my mind that, come what way, I will be satisfied with where God leads me. I must say that most days I have to override my feelings and plan deliberately to have a good day. Once I've made this decision, it changes my whole attitude. Remember all battles begin in your mind. When you decide to have a good day and follow through, it won't be long until you are truly having a great day and you even feel good in your body.

9. Obey God. I not only ask God for His guidance but I purpose in my heart to be obedient to Him. What happens when your friend Sue runs up to you and asks your opinion about what she should do or how she should respond in a situation? You think about what would be best and give her your honest opinion. Sue turns around and does something totally different. Not only that, she makes a huge mess out of it. You think, *Wow, why did she ask my opinion and then totally ignore it? If she has such a low regard for my opinion, next time I won't have an opinion. Why waste my breath?* I hope God doesn't think of me that way. I thank Him for His patience and graciousness and kindness and help. I believe it gives Him joy to help me.

10. End your prayer with praise. There is so much to praise God for! He has worked out many impossible situations in our lives. He has parted the Red Sea as we walked through on dry land. He has provided finances when we thought we would not make it through the month. He is our protector. He is our shelter and strong tower, our shield and buckler. It is appropriate that God's children end their prayer time with thanks and praise. It sets the tone and mood for the day. "Praise Him for His mighty acts. Praise Him according to His excellent greatness!" (Psalm 150:2).

Distance, Distractions, Time, and Place

Distance: If at some point in your life you feel God has distanced Himself from you, remember this: He hasn't moved; you're the one who has moved. I know this because God is omnipresent, and we always have direct access to Him anytime we need Him. "In him we live, and move, and have our being. . . . For through Him we both have access by one spirit to the Father" (Acts 17:28; Ephesians 2:18, KJV). Never forget that! Even when it seems He is a million miles away, God is right there.

Distractions: It never fails. Every time we get down to pray there is a distraction, whether internal or external. Our mind will transport us to crazy places if we let it. We have to learn how to block the hindering thoughts. Have you ever said to yourself, "I just can't get it out of my mind"? I have. Sometimes we act as if we are helpless human beings that have no control over our minds. We give in too easily. As we will discuss in chapter 10, we have to learn to take every thought captive. It takes time and work, but it can be done.

Time and Place: You need to pick a time and place that will invite as few distractions as possible. I have prayed in many places besides my "prayer closet," although I think you should have a special, designated place you can go to first thing in the morning. Beyond that, the Scripture tells us to "pray without ceasing." That means continuously. You may ask, "How can I do that? I've got work, family, church activities and services, and friends to think of." I believe as we go through our day we should always have our heart and mind open to God's voice and prompting. Many times after the initial hour of prayer we jump up to start the day's activities and shut our mind and heart off to God. It doesn't have to be that way. In fact, it shouldn't be that way. That is the beauty of it. You don't have to be in one certain place or time for Him to speak to you. He walks with you throughout the day, speaking awesome, encouraging words to you—like when you are hearing a not-so-good medical report or having trouble with your next door neighbor. God sends tests your way. You just have to keep your ears open to His still, small voice.

I remember the days I fought to have the right thought process. I was so desperate I would scream, "Please help me, God! Give me an understanding of this situation!" Many times a rift would open up in the clouds and all of a sudden I would see what I couldn't see just minutes before. Eventually I learned that if I didn't get an immediate answer, God would come through in due time. Sure enough, as I kept my heart and ears open to Him, He would give me the answer I needed.

I believe it was prayer that saved me from having an addiction. Most people who suffer from Borderline Personality Disorder have a co-occurring addiction. I would cycle, and at the point things got desperate, instead of getting drunk or high on drugs, I would get in my car and drive until I found a quiet place to park and cry out to God. I didn't know anything about BPD; I just knew that without God's help I would go crazy.

If only people would choose in the beginning to go to God for help instead of waiting until they are at the end of their rope, addiction might not be an obstacle. Too often we wait until we are at a loss before we turn to God.

Sometimes instead of turning to God we turn to our friends for answers. This can be helpful if we approach it in the right way and if we are also getting help from God. Sometimes if we reveal what God is putting on our heart, our friends and family can help us piece the puzzle together. Don't ever leave God out of the equation.

Can you think of times you should have gone to God about your problem but you didn't? Think about it and then summarize what you could have done better.

1. _____

2. _____

3. _____

4. _____

5. _____

6. _____

Here are some changes I had to make in order to grow and communicate with God in the right way.

1. I learned it was not all about feelings when I prayed. God could hear and answer my prayer even if I didn't feel goose bumps scampering up and down my spine.
2. I learned I must pray every day whether I felt like it or not.
3. I learned through revelation and experience that God is my friend.
4. I learned that God always hears my prayers.

I want you to look at your prayer life and see where you can improve in your time, thoughts, and actions. Then try to implement these strategies in your life.

1. _____

2. _____

3. _____

4. _____

5. _____

6. _____

If God could help me improve in these areas, I believe He can and will help you as well. No matter how many times you have tried before, don't ever give up. Soon you will discover what prayer can do!

Chapter 9

Bible Reading and Meditation

To be honest, reading the Bible is one thing I always struggled with. I didn't have trouble with praying, but to sit down and read my Bible was a struggle. I have since realized that I must change my attitude and the way I think.

"Thy word is a lamp unto my feet, and a light unto my path" (Psalm 119:105, KJV). How can we possibly see which way to go without a lamp? God is our light and our salvation. I have become passionate about God's Word. What I have experienced through reading the Bible has opened my understanding.

One thing I have discovered about God's Word is that many of His promises are conditional. God does not automatically drop everything into our lap. For instance, here's one of my favorite passages:

> Finally brethren, whatever things are true, whatever things are noble, whatever things are just, whatever things are pure, whatever things are lovely, whatever things are of good report, if there is any virtue and if there is anything praiseworthy—meditate on these things. The things which you learned and received and heard and saw in me, these do, and the God of peace will be with you. (Philippians 4:8–9)

God doesn't just arbitrarily open the window of heaven and pour a bucket of peace over our heads. But we will have peace when we "think on these things." Notice that all the things on the above list are good things—good for our minds. They are positive and upbeat. God is drawn to us when we are thinking about miracles, healings, or good things about our friends and family. God loves being close to us when we are thinking on these things. It brings joy both to His heart and ours. It brings the love and peace of God.

Yes, you are human. You have bad days. Some mornings you get up on the wrong side of the bed, and as the day wears on, things go from bad to worse. What do you think about throughout the day? Finding the kitchen sink all clogged up and the huge bill the plumber hands you after he removes the clog. Little Sally in the checkout line at Kroger reaches for a candy display and the whole display ends up on the floor. Someone behind you says, "Slobs!" You think about the note Johnny's teacher sends home from school complaining about his bad behavior. After dinner your husband Lester says the pork chops are dry. Then you wonder where the peace went. Well, there's no need to wonder. Whose day wouldn't get worse when they're meditating on things like that?

It's so lovely when we can pick up God's Word and find a quiet place to read and meditate on His promises and precepts. There is nothing like having the God of peace sitting beside you!

Jesus assured believers, "If you abide in My word, you are My disciples indeed. And you shall know the truth, and the truth shall make you free" (John 8:31–32). If you are His disciple, you will abide in His Word. His Word is truth, and the truth shall make you free. Reading the newspaper won't make you free. Spending three hours on social media won't make you free. Watching a movie won't make you free. Gossiping on the phone won't make you free. And certainly, believing Satan's lies won't make you free. The only thing that will free you is delving into the truth of God's Word and believing it with all of your heart.

I believe the reason we don't see the truth is because *we don't want to see it*. We don't want to see it because then we would be compelled to act upon it. In I Timothy 4, Paul gave his son in the gospel a whole list of things to do, like nourishing himself in the word of faith, rejecting old wives' tales, being an example to others in conduct and word, and giving attention to reading the Word and exhortation. Then he wrote, "Meditate on these things; give yourself entirely to them, that your progress may be evident to all" (I Timothy 4:15). The word *meditate* in this verse denotes attending to, or practicing what has been presented.

Once you see the truth in God's Word, you must do something about it if you expect the truth to make you free. When you see where you were wrong in your thinking or actions, you have to choose to change. Your desire and determination has to go way down deep in the uttermost part of your heart. You must let it touch your spirit. There are too many people who are know-it-alls. They can tell you just how things are supposed to be, but they themselves don't do it. The truth has not sunk deep into their spirit yet. They have not embraced it. You must be desperate enough and to the point your heart is open and you are ready to embrace the truth.

The truth is that God is your Healer and Deliverer. You can overcome anything if you are walking with the mind of Christ. Don't let Satan tell you otherwise.

> For the word of God is living and powerful, and sharper than any two-edged sword, piercing even to the division of soul and spirit, and of joints and marrow, and is a discerner of the thoughts and intents of the heart. . . . Let us therefore come boldly to the throne of grace that we may obtain mercy and find grace to help in the time of need. (Hebrews 4:12, 16)

When He walked in the earth, Jesus was as human as we are and experienced everything that we experience. He knows how painful it is to look at the truth. As they say, "Truth hurts!"

> An amazing fact of the Christian faith is that the infinite God became a finite human being. Although without sin, Jesus Christ as a man experienced the weakness, temptations, pain, and difficulties of a human existence. Thus, we have a Savior who can sympathize with our weaknesses. He understands temptation, because He faced it. He understands weakness, because He experienced it. He understands pain, because He felt it. (The Soul Care Bible, Tim Clinton, ed., p. 1624)

> This hope we have as an anchor of the soul, both sure and steadfast. (Hebrews 6:29)

The Bible is full of instructions on how to conduct ourselves. I want you to take time and think. Has God been trying to show you a revelation as you read the Bible? Have you seen some truths that you are too afraid to embrace because they will require a major change? What are they?

1. _____

2. _____

3. _____

4. _____

5. _____

6. _____

You can read certain verses over and over again and think there is no more to glean from them. Then all of a sudden a deeper meaning jumps out at you like lightning. God has shown you something you have never noticed before.

How are you doing presently with your Bible reading? What do you struggle with? Write down your thoughts and feelings.

1. _____

2. _____

3. _____

4. _____

5. _____

6. _____

When I started reading the Bible consistently, I had a hard time focusing my attention. *I need pictures,* I thought. *I want a story!* Then I tried The Message. I do not recommend it for doctrinal study, but it is good at laying out a scriptural story line that is easy to understand.

There are many other translations we can glean from as well. In short, it is best to base everything on the King James Version and use other translations to shed additional light for better comprehension.

Borderlines struggle with Bible study. They are all about feelings, and if the passage they are reading isn't helping them with their feelings, the Bible-reading will quickly get shoved to the back burner.

Let me encourage you to read the Bible. So many times I have been at my wits' end and contemplating giving up. What good was I to anybody anyway? Then I would muster up enough determination to go to a quiet room and open my Bible. I read Psalm 27 so many times that the Bible usually fell open to it: "The LORD is my light and my salvation: whom shall I fear? The LORD is the strength of my life; of whom shall I be afraid?" (v.1). I could feel Jesus coming ever so close to me.

> Hear, O LORD, when I cry with my voice! Have mercy also upon me, and answer me. When You said, "Seek My face," my heart said to You, "Your face, LORD, I will seek." Do not hide Your face from me; do not turn Your servant away in anger; You have been my help; do not leave me nor forsake me, O God of my salvation. (Psalm 27:7–9)

God would always answer my cries. You see, sometimes it's hard to find the words to express what you are feeling—what you need from God. But every time you open the Bible, it will calm your spirit. It is like a soothing salve on a wound. It is like a sip of iced tea in the middle of July. He will be your ever-present help with whatever you need at that moment.

The Bible will give you a solid foundation on which to stand. I remember how much I enjoyed hearing the late Priscilla McGruder tell of the times when she was suffering with her health. She would get the Bible, lay it on the floor, place her feet upon the Word, and say, "I am standing on the Word!" When she didn't know what else to do, she could stand upon the Word and know everything would be all right. Thank You, Jesus!

If we truly want to be healed and made whole, we must fall in love with God's Word. Reading the Word is the only way our mind can be transformed. It takes our flighty, make-believe thought patterns and grounds them in truth. It will renew our inner man day by day. It will tell us how God thinks. Then it will help us to think as God thinks.

> And be not conformed to this world: but be ye transformed by the renewing of your mind, that ye may prove what is that good, and acceptable, and perfect will of God. (Romans 12:2, KJV)

> For which cause we faint not; but though our outward man perish, yet the inward man is renewed day by day. (II Corinthians 4:16, KJV)

Meditation

To meditate means to think deeply and carefully about something, to ponder or imagine. Go to the Book of Psalms for a list of things to think about:

1. The works of God (77:12; 143:5)
2. The precepts and ways of God (119:15, 78)
3. The statutes of God ("My hands also I will lift up to Your commandments, which I love, and I will meditate on your statutes [119:48])
4. The Word of God (119:148).

What are you meditating on? Think back: what do you meditate on most in your down time?

1. _____

2. _____

3. _____

4. _____

5. _____

What you allow your mind to dwell on is very important because meditating on the right things will bring healing to your mind. Therefore, be careful what you read and think about. "Then [Jesus] said to them, 'Take heed what you hear. With the same measure you use, it will be measured to you; and to you who hear, more will be given'" (Mark 4:24). This is an awesome verse of Scripture! It tells us that the more time we spend reading and meditating on the Word of God the more good things we will reap.

The psalmist said he spent a lot of time thinking about the Word of God: "I will meditate on your precepts, and contemplate Your ways" (Psalm 119:15). You can't meditate on the Word of God if you don't read it. The more time you spend reading and thinking about the precepts and ways of God, the more ability and power you will have to do what it says.

Many times throughout the day, my mind goes back to a verse I have read that morning. Then God gives me light and revelation about that verse. It is exhilarating! When this happens, you know God is watching over you and helping you to grow and heal. Isn't it awesome when He takes the time to show you something? You are important to Him; He cares about you and your well-being. He wants you to prosper and grow in your walk with Him.

"We have thought, O God, on Your lovingkindness, in the midst of Your temple" (Psalm 48:9). Never forget your mind plays a big role in your healing and your victory. It rejuvenates your spirit when you take a moment to think back about all that God has done for you, from the big things to the little things. Here is an example:

I had always wanted to try my hand at fixing a prime rib roast, but it was too expensive for our budget. Nevertheless, I mentioned my wish to various people in passing conversation: "One of these days, when I get the money, I'm going to fix a prime rib!" Not one time did I ever dream anything would come of it.

The church where my daughter and son-in-law attend do a food pantry several times a month. Wouldn't you know, a prime rib roast came through and they brought it over to my house. I was so excited! It wasn't just a run-of-the-mill piece of meat; it was a high-quality roast with no artificial additives. I cooked it for our Easter dinner and it turned out perfectly!

To some it may seem like a little thing, but to me it was special. I believe it was God's way of telling me He cares. It's one of the little things I can meditate on.

I want you to meditate on some good things God has done in your life, even if they seem insignificant:

1. _____

2. _____

3. _____

4. _____

5. _____

6. _____

I believe some people can't connect with God's Word because they are thinking with a carnal mind. No wonder they're discouraged and can't get out of the dumps. They're operating on a carnal level, trying to figure out everything on their own instead of delving into the Word of God for answers.

It is possible to keep your mind set on positive things and the goodness of Jesus. Specifics on how to do this will be covered in another chapter, but for now I'll say these are things that will help you grow and succeed in life. Don't sit there thinking you can't help yourself. Yes, you can!

For one thing, if your mind is occupied by good and positive things, you won't have time to brood about unfortunate situations. This will work even if you are contending with BPD or any other emotional or personality disorder. Don't automatically say you can't do this. Yes, you can! You can do it by pushing forward in your healing a little bit at a time. I know because I did it. God can and will help you, but you have to be willing to do your part. He will not force you to meditate on good things. He created you with your own free will, and you must choose whether or not you will do His will.

In the space provided below, write some things you want to meditate on that are praiseworthy and beneficial to your spirit. Purpose in your heart to follow through.

1. _____

2. _____

3. _____

4. _____

5. _____

6. _____

Let us meditate on good things. It will make us strong through Jesus Christ!

Chapter 10

Take Every Thought Captive and Change the Way You Think

And be not conformed to this world: but be ye transformed by the renewing of your mind, that ye may prove what is that good, and acceptable, and perfect, will of God. (Romans 12:2, KJV)

Are you ready to change the way you think? It will change your life! Besides Bible reading and prayer time, I feel this is one of the most important steps toward healing: learning to take every thought captive! I'm not saying it is easy; it is probably one of the hardest things to conquer, especially for a Borderline. God helped me to master this as little by little I learned to reprogram my thoughts. During a session, I would tell Vani, my counselor, "I understand the facts about this and how to think about it correctly." Vani would exclaim, "Jodie! That's a miracle!" It is a miracle, because people with BPD are incapable of seeing this; they cannot tell if the constant stream of "self-talk" is real or imaginary.

Luke 6:45 says, "A good man out of the good treasure of his heart brings forth good; and an evil man out of the evil treasure of his heart brings forth evil. For out of the abundance of the heart his mouth speaks." When you change the way you think, it will change the way you talk.

You will need a special person to help you reprogram your thoughts, someone with whom you can talk things out. As we discussed in chapter 2, this person is the anchor of your support team. He or she will recognize whether or not you are thinking straight, and will be able to correct you when you go off track. Together you can change the way you think.

Learning to take every thought captive and run it by the Bible is like making new tracks in your mind. This statement has a scientific base in that the human brain has "plasticity"; it keeps changing throughout a person's lifetime. As early as 1949, psychology professor Donald Olding Hebb discovered that connections between neurons that are frequently activated will become stronger. Those that exchange little information will become weaker (*Science Daily*, 10 October 2013). In other words, when you make new tracks—new connections—the old, unused ones will weaken and disappear. That is only one of the reasons why I'm convinced you can learn how to think differently!

I remember that when I started thinking differently not only my conversation changed, but my actions began to change as well. It was as if I became a new person, and in reality, I was! People who had known me before weren't expecting me to react in these new, healthy ways. When they noticed the difference, I felt so good. I felt transformed. Granted, it took quite a while; reprogramming is a slow process. But when I finally succeeded, I hardly recognized myself. I was overwhelmed with joy!

Following is a list of quotations from various Bible versions to add depth of meaning to Romans 12:2:

1. "Be transformed and progressively changed [as you mature spiritually] by the renewing of your mind [focusing on godly values and ethical attitudes], so that you may prove [for yourselves] what the will of God is, that which is good and acceptable and perfect [in His plan and purpose for you]" (Romans 12:2, AMP).
2. "Don't be like the people of this world, but let God change the way you think. Then you will know how to do everything that is good and pleasing to Him" (Romans 12:2, CEV).
3. "Let God change you inside with a new way of thinking" (Romans 12:2, ERV).
4. "Let God re-mould your minds from within so that you may prove in practice that the plan of God for you is good" (Romans 12:2, Phillips).

You must take every thought captive. And don't wait until thirty thoughts have zoomed through our mind. If you do, you will become overwhelmed and give up.

Write down some things you now realize you need to stop thinking about.

1. _____

2. _____

3. _____

4. _____

5. _____

6. _____

> For the weapons of our warfare are not carnal but mighty in God for pulling down strongholds, casting down arguments [imaginations, KJV] and every high thing that exalts itself against the knowledge of God, bringing every thought into captivity to the obedience of Christ. (II Corinthians 10:4–5)

You must learn to capture every thought and weigh it on the balance scale of God's Word. Does this thought tip the scale toward the biblical way of thinking? Or does it instead weigh heavier on the side of Satan or your flesh? If it is not in agreement with the Word of God, get rid of it! It does not belong in your mind. The longer you let it stay the harder it is to get rid of it. Cast it out!

It may sound humorous, but I came against wrong thinking by talking to myself. If you say your thoughts out loud, you sometimes realize how foolish they sound. You need to get the foolish thoughts out of your head and out of your mouth. As long as you keep them in your mind, the thoughts will grow bigger and reproduce. I would sometimes plead that God would cover my mind with His blood, and the thoughts would leave instantly.

In my experience, if a thought is negative, most likely it isn't from God. Even when God is trying to work on your heart and show you what you did wrong or where you failed, He uses encouragement and love to motivate you to do the right thing. He is pushing you uphill, not downhill.

I am not minimizing the hurts you have encountered in the past. People can be cruel and can say hurtful things. But are you helping yourself by replaying and re-thinking their wrong actions and the hurt they inflicted? No! That track goes only one way—down. In those times you must deliberately say, "No, I refuse to think about this anymore!" Then, on purpose, through sheer willpower, think on good things!

We discussed Bible reading in chapter 9, but I would like to return to it. It's a superb and very effective way of casting unhealthy thoughts out of your mind. Many times when I was desperate to get my thinking back on track, I would grab my Bible and head to a quiet room, sit down in a comfortable chair, and start reading. It would sometimes take a while, but pretty soon the Word would put me back on track and bring me comfort and peace that passes all understanding.

This may sound a little forceful, but do not make excuses for yourself. When your thoughts run amok, don't allow yourself to say, "I just can't help it!" God gave you the tools that will fix the problem. I know you can do this because God helped me do it. Get a good grip on the encouraging Scripture passages below.

1. "I can do all things through Christ who strengthens me" (Philippians 4:13).
2. "Let this mind be in you which was also in Christ Jesus" (Philippians 2:5).
3. "Do you not know that you are the temple of God and that the spirit of God dwells in you?" (I Corinthians 3:16).

The Spirit of God dwells in you. You are not some little weakling that is tossed to and fro by every wind (or thought) that tries to breach the gates of your mind. No! You are a child of the King; you have royal blood in your veins; you have been bought with a price. Therefore, you can conquer the enemy and acquire a new, positive, Christlike way of thinking. The whole world will recognize the difference in you. They will know Christ is living inside of you.

Finally brethren, whatever things are true, whatever things are noble, whatever things are just, whatever things are pure, whatever things are lovely, whatever things are of good report, if there is any virtue and if there is anything praiseworthy—meditate on these things. The things which you learned and received and heard and saw in me, these do, and the God of peace will be with you. (Philippians 4:8–9)

This verse says so much, but it is so familiar that I think we sometimes read it then let it drop. We say, "That's nice. I think that would be good for everybody to do." Unfortunately, we never make the effort to put it into practice because it is a lot of work! But I want to tell you that it is hard work that pays fantastic dividends. Would you like to go through the day with peace and no worry? You can. But you have to work at it every day. It has to become your lifestyle, the way you live every day. It needs to become as common as eating three meals a day. After a while it will become natural to you, and you will then have "the mind of Christ."

Thus far, this chapter has focused on changing your thought patterns. I would like to use the remainder of the chapter to highlight certain areas of and influences on your thought life: fear and effect, tiredness and self-talk, context and relationships, wandering thoughts, trusting your own reasoning, and worry and anxiety.

Fear and Effect

For God has not given us a spirit of fear, but of power and of love and of a sound mind. (II Timothy 1:7)

Fear is a horrible thing. Fear can be all-consuming. It can paralyze you. It can make your behavior irrational. Your body undergoes a huge adrenalin rush. Your heart rate speeds up; your blood pressure soars; your breathing goes shallow and rapid; you break out in a sweat. I want to assure you that this kind of fear is not of God.

The flip-side is that we have natural fears—things we *should* be afraid of, such as dangerous animals, fire, tornadoes—in short, things that could harm us. God gave us those fears in order to protect us. The type of all-consuming fear mentioned above, however, can be cruel and exhausting. I have seen people who are overrun by fear.

I have always had a fear of water. Many years ago, I went with some friends to Branson, Missouri. We were having a great time when they all decided we should go on a waterslide. I was afraid, but I didn't want to be a party pooper. We got in the queue and waited—and waited—and waited. The longer we stood there the more terrified I got. When we finally reached the front of the line, they told us everyone had to go down the slide head first. That was even more terrifying!

Gingerly, I positioned myself on the mat they provided, and down I went, scared to the bone. After navigating all the twists and turns, I came to the end, a three-foot-deep pool—but I didn't know that. By then I had lost all common sense and reason. I shot into the pool, went under, and did not come back up. I stayed underwater so long the guard at the edge of the pool became concerned and moved to assist me. You see, all I had to do was stand up. But I was paralyzed by fear and had to be helped out of the water. When my friends realized how scared I was, they felt bad. The personnel refunded my money, and I sat there waiting on my friends until they were done. I remember feeling ridiculous, but that didn't alleviate my natural fear of water.

I have seen some people make horrible decisions and choices while in a fearful state. You should never make any kind of important decision when gripped by fear, because fear makes it impossible to think straight. Your decision could prove to be fatal.

Faith and fear cannot coexist in your heart. Yes, there will be times when you are hanging on to faith by a thread. I realize you cannot walk in continuous faith every waking moment. This is where Bible reading and prayer are so valuable because reading the Bible and praying in faith work together in perfect harmony to alleviate fear.

When you become fearful you must cast it out. Fear will hinder you only as long as you hang on to it. Give it to God. He does a much better job with fearful situations than we do.

Write down some of the things you are afraid of:

1. _____

2. _____

3. _____

4. _____

5. _____

6. _____

Sickness, Tiredness, and Self-talk

Satan will attack your mind in the most vulnerable areas, and he knows the opportune time to strike—when you're sick and tired. If you wake up sick and struggling, don't get upset and give up; just realize when you are at your weakest, God is at His strongest for you. Don't beat yourself up because you don't feel like you're doing well. You are just tired and sick. The devil is mean and cruel and has no mercy. In vulnerable moments like this you must be aware of your adversary. You are not ignorant of his devices, so be prepared and proactive. You can beat him at his own game.

At times I have been so tired I couldn't think straight. When you are tired, your concentration and response time is off, and you are more irritable and sensitive. That's a prime time to watch carefully what you say and do. It is all too easy to wound someone because you don't feel well. In moments like these, running your thoughts by someone on your support team can be very helpful. Just keep in mind that you are sensitive and you might get your feelings hurt. Borderlines are especially susceptible to this type of situation, so remember not to let your feelings run your life.

> *"The key to changing the way we think, the way we feel, and the way we behave is changing the stories we tell ourselves!"* Mark Batterson

The wrong brand of self-talk can get you into a lot of trouble if you let it. If your self-talk is truthful and positive, you will be fine, but if your self-talk is make-believe and negative, it is setting you up for failure. You must tell yourself the right story. The true story. Eugene Peterson said, "Feelings don't run the show. There is a reality deeper than our feelings. Live by that."

Taking every thought captive involves not only telling yourself the right story, but being able to stick with it through thick and thin. No matter what happens to you throughout the day or how disappointed you are with yourself, keep telling yourself the right story!

My story is that I have been forgiven, and His Spirit lives inside of me. God loves me and cares for me every day. He's as close as the mention of His name. I was created by God. God healed me and delivered me from BPD. I am on my way to heaven to see my Jesus face to face. This is just a small sample of my story to help you get started.

Write down your story. Keep it in front of you every day! It's the truth.

_____

_____

_____

_____

Have you ever heard someone who, even though they didn't have the whole story, wanted to believe the event happened a certain way? Their mind is made up; there is no convincing them it happened any other way. Anything positive they hear, they will give it a negative spin so it will fit into their narrative. This is the case largely because admitting their story is wrong means they will have to eat their words. Their pride won't let them change their story. They would have too much restitution and reconciliation to do. Don't spend time around people like these. Hang around people who have a true story and are sticking to it. Likewise, you can encourage others by the word of your testimony. Having a true story builds your faith and the faith of those who hear what God has done for you. He has brought you a mighty long way!

You will keep him in perfect peace, whose mind is stayed on You, because he trusts in You. Trust in the

LORD forever, for in YAH, the LORD, is everlasting strength. (Isaiah 26:3–4)

Depression is sometimes caused by a chemical imbalance that requires medication, and, in some cases, medication helps. But by and large, people who are depressed are telling themselves the wrong story. This is because the thoughts a person allows their mind to dwell on will come out in their behavior and ultimately lead to the outcome of their life. Have you ever been around someone who is depressed and listened to what they are saying? Most of the time they don't want encouragement; they want you to agree with how bad they have it because that will validate what they believe. It gives them an excuse to be and stay depressed. I know because I have been depressed in the past, and it's a horrible place to be. If you are suffering from depression, the last person you need to talk to is the person who feeds your depression.

Context and Relationships

By *context* I mean the "interrelated conditions in which something exists or occurs: environment, setting (*Merriam-Webster's Collegiate Dictionary*). Context is important. I have already touched on this area, but it is so important I want to reemphasize it. As we are learning to take every thought captive, it is very important to be aware of our context—the cognitive climate swirling around us. Who do you like to hang out with? What are your favorite haunts? If you are constantly surrounding yourself with negative people, they will drag you, along with your thinking, down to their level.

Jim Rohn, entrepreneur and motivational speaker, said, "You are the average of the five people you spend the most time with." This is because the more time you spend hobnobbing with certain people, the more influence they have on you, and you eventually begin to act, speak, and think like them. So context can either bring you down or elevate you.

I will concede that sometimes you have to be in a negative context. That's when it's important to plead the blood of Jesus over your mind. Ask God to cover it with protection. With His strength, the negativity won't have much effect on you.

117

Name a place or places you have to be sometimes when you really need to plead the blood over your mind.

1. _____

2. _____

3. _____

4. _____

5. _____

6. _____

Wandering Thoughts

Another thing to resist is letting your thoughts wander at will. You can discipline your thoughts, the same as you can discipline your actions. I'm talking about *self-discipline*. Have you ever been sitting in church listening to the preacher and all of a sudden your mind drifts off in another direction? Eventually you tune back into the same wavelength as the preacher, but by then you have no idea what he has been saying. What about in conversation? Do you lose concentration while listening to someone talk? It's easy to do. We must learn not to let our minds wander at will. The devil knows if we have a wandering mind. And when we give him the foothold of wandering thoughts, he will take unfair advantage of it.

Trusting Our Own Reasoning

I understand that everyday activities and goals need to be planned out. Try going grocery shopping and cooking dinner from scratch without any planning. Try hosting an annual church event or taking students on a field trip without any planning. Try writing a research paper or getting all of your homework done on time without planning. Some things just won't get done unless we plan.

What I'm talking about here is when this type of planning is taken farther than God ever intended for it to go. I'm talking about planning and reasoning to the extent that we have everything figured out; we don't need to consult God. We can get so dependent on our own reasoning that we don't feel we need anyone else. How much better it is when we learn to work alongside of God! He has a perfect plan for everything we do, and a master plan for our lives.

Another drawback of depending on our own reasoning is that it tends to make us hard of hearing when God is trying to communicate with us. We worry the problem like a dog gnawing at a bone until we reason it to death and completely miss the wonderful things God has in store. There are other times when God impresses us to do something, but it makes no sense to us. It doesn't sound reasonable. Should we do it or not? Go ahead. His thoughts are on a much higher plane than ours. He can see way down the road, whereas we see only the next step.

Try it. Next time you are facing an impossibility or have a need, instead of figuring it out from every angle, take it to God. Will His plan look just like yours? Probably not. But it will be the best plan, and it will generate the best outcome.

> Trust in the Lord with all your heart, and lean not on your own understanding; in all your ways acknowledge Him, and He shall direct your paths. (Proverbs 3:5–6)

> For the LORD gives wisdom; from His mouth come knowledge and understanding; He stores up sound wisdom for the upright; He is a shield for those who walk uprightly. . . . Wisdom enters your heart, and knowledge is pleasant to your soul. (Proverbs 2:6–7, 10)

Are you currently putting everything in God's hands? What are some things you need to give to God?

1. _____

2. _____

3. _____

4. _____

5. _____

6. _____

Putting everything in God's hands will help you sleep better at night. Although there are medical reasons why we sometimes don't sleep well, I believe more often than not we go to bed pondering everything we need to do and snatch it right back out of God's hands. I have spent many sleepless nights, and it is not worth it! It doesn't take long to enter a continuous cycle of insomnia, and when you are sleep-deprived, you can't think clearly the next day—and once you get on this merry-go-round, it's extremely hard to get off! Does this sound familiar?

Worry and Anxiety

The last ugly emotion I want to bring to you is worry and anxiety. Psalm 37:8 says, "Fret not thyself in any wise." When the enemy attacks your mind with worry and anxiety, you won't be able to think clearly.

I used to be a bundle of anxiety; I was incapable of making decisions about *anything*. My thought process was thrown off balance, which siphoned me into a downward spiral. I thought if I could run from everything, then everything would somehow get fixed. This was unreasonable, but BPD held the reins of my mind and it seemed I couldn't help myself. People with addictions find themselves in the same helpless predicament. They're desperate to control their anxieties so they run to their choice fix, whether it be drugs, alcohol, shopping, working, or gambling. Then when or if they get free of the addiction, they still have a lot of damage control to do.

Actually, worrying is believing God cannot handle our situation! Have you ever seen a bird sitting on a power line while having a nervous breakdown because he doesn't know where his next meal is coming from? Of course not; that's ridiculous. God feeds the birds. If God takes care of the sparrows, then he is more than able to take care of you! To think that He won't answer your prayers or take care of your dilemma is a faulty thinking pattern. It's even worse when you think you can do a better job than God!

When I learned to think about things that are pure, lovely, and of a good report, when I taught myself to think about how great God is and how far He has brought me, it made it easy to believe God can do anything. God has totally turned my life around! He took what surely would have been a disaster and turned it into a testimony! Out of the void of my worst-case scenario He created a miracle!

Let God do the same for you. He will be your Healer and Deliverer. He will help you take every thought captive, and in the process you will be set free!

Chapter 11

The Powerful Spoken Word

> *Death and life are in the power of the tongue; and those who love it will eat its fruit. (Proverbs 18:21)*

The above verse in The Message reads, "Words kill, words give life; they're either poison or fruit—you choose." There is more power in the tiny muscles of the tongue than in any other muscle in the body. Many people do not realize the impact of the words coming out of their mouth. Words can tear down or build up. Words can destroy or create. Words can imprison or set free. Therefore, the words we speak must be intentional. We must take care to filter our words through the Word of God. If we change the way we speak, we can change the way we think and vice versa. That's the power of the spoken word!

My brethren, be not many masters, knowing that we shall receive the greater condemnation. For in many things we offend all. If any man offend not in word, the same is a perfect man, and able also to bridle the whole body. Behold, we put bits in the horses' mouths, that they may obey us; and we turn about their whole body. Behold also the ships, which though they be so great, and are driven of fierce winds, yet are they turned about with a very small helm, withersoever the governor listeth. Even so the tongue is a little member, and boasteth great things. Behold, how great a matter a little fire kindleth! And the tongue is a fire, a world of iniquity: so is the tongue among our members, that it defileth the whole body, and setteth on fire the course of nature; and it is set on fire of hell. For every kind of beast, and of birds, and of serpents, and of things in the sea, is tamed, and hath been tamed of mankind: but the tongue can no man tame; it is an unruly evil, full of deadly poison. (James 3:1–7, KJV)

When I look back at the many words I let fly, I cringe. Unbeknownst to me, I was letting Borderline Personality Disorder run my life, but that is no excuse. Yes, God has forgiven me, and apologies and restitution have been made, but I can never obliterate those words from anyone's mind, including my own. I am left hoping the people I said those words to will choose not to remember them or let anything I said sway their opinions of me.

Think back to the times you have heard something negative about somebody, even though you suspected it wasn't true. You shove it to the back of your mind, but you can't completely forget it. Those words will tend to sway your opinion even if it's only by a small percentage. We must never say anything about somebody that is negative or false no matter how small or insignificant it may seem to us. Words can come back to haunt us. We can wish a million times we never said them, but by then it's too late.

Many times we say negative things about ourselves that aren't true. Here are some of my personal examples:

1. "I'm never going to get better!"
2. "I'm so stupid."
3. "I will never be a good wife or mother."
4. "I am useless."

What are some of the negative things you have said about yourself that aren't really true?

1. _____

2. _____

3. _____

4. _____

5. _____

You need to realize that if you keep telling yourself these false things, you will end up believing them. You are telling yourself a bad story, feeding false data into your mind-bank that will bring you down. Not only that, when you speak those negative words out loud, the spirit world hears what you say. You are informing the devil of the optimum place—your weakest place—to attack you. You are handing him the tools to plan his strategy and the weapons to destroy you, or at least hinder you.

James was right: you have the power of life and death in your tongue. David told us what to do about it when he said, "I will guard my ways, lest I sin with my tongue; I will restrain my mouth with a muzzle, while the wicked are before me" (Psalm 39:1). It is vital that we watch the words that come out of our mouth.

Dr. Sharon R. Bonds, PhD, offers a further consideration: "Words have energy vibrations and spirits attached to them that affects [*sic*] both the sender and the receiver while opening up vibrations that invoke feelings and emotions into the recipients and those spirits are invoked by the providers' intent" ("The Power of the Spoken Word: Words Like Thoughts Have Molding Power," https://www.allaboutloveinc.org/About Me.en.html). Bonds goes on to say:

> Our bodies are made mostly of energy and water, which makes us the conductors of energy. Imagine the impact of our thoughts and words on our health. Now if words have an energy base and that base affect[s] our health, then it means that negative, unforgiving thoughts would be the seat of most sickness and cancers. Energy flows easily between people . . . how are we affecting those around us?

Our thoughts come out in our speech. Through our speech (language) we understand and regulate our actions and our interactions with other people. It is interesting that the frontal lobe, where the center of speech is located, also controls motor behavior (body movement). Messages zoom from neurons and synapses in the brain to all parts of the body via the spinal cord, and back again. Thus everything about our body is interconnected (i.e., our thoughts, speech or words, motor behavior, interactions with others, and the effect of these on ourselves and others).

That's why I say the tongue may be the least member of our body, but it can steer the whole body. When you vocalize, "I have no ability; I can't do this job," you have just sent an instant message to the central nervous system that you have no abilities, so striving to be capable of doing the job is useless. Your speech can set your whole body up for success or failure.

Some years back I knew a man who watched his mother die of cancer. On the way home from the cemetery he said to his wife, "I'll probably die of cancer too." From that point on he was convinced he had cancer. Doctors kept reassuring him there was no sign of the feared disease, but unfortunately, they eventually did find a tumor and the man died within a year of his mother's passing.

Have you ever heard somebody say with a hangdog look, "I'm going to flunk this test. I don't know the material." Then they pass with flying colors and bounce out of the room saying, "I knew I was going to pass that test! I'm smart and I studied hard." No, if they've gone into the classroom with a defeatist attitude, they usually fail the test and come out saying, "I knew I wasn't going to pass. I'm too stupid!" It is no surprise that people who are confident and positive most of the time usually achieve their goals. Likewise, it is no surprise that people who are down-in-the-mouth, discouraged, and unhappy most of the time usually do not achieve their goals, that is, if they had any in the first place!

Death and life are in the power of the tongue, and those who love it will eat its fruit. Proverbs 18:21

Here is proof of the power of the spoken word: ten different times as God was creating the heavens and the earth, He spoke and it was so:

1. Genesis 1:3 – "Let there be light: and there was light."
2. Genesis 1:6 – "Let there be a firmament . . . and it was so."
3. Genesis 1:9 – "Let the waters be gathered and let dry land appear: and it was so."
4. Genesis 1:11 – "Let the earth bring forth vegetation: and it was so."

5. Genesis 1:14 – "Let there be lights in the firmament: and it was so."
6. Genesis 1:20 – "Let the waters bring forth abundantly, and it was so."
7. Genesis 1:24 – "Let the earth bring forth living creatures: and it was so."
8. Genesis 1:26 – "Let us make man in our image . . . and man became a living soul."
9. Genesis 1:28, 30 – "Be fruitful and multiply, and replenish the earth, and subdue it . . . and it was so."
10. Genesis 1:29 – "I have given you every herb and every tree for food: and it was so."

God spoke, and all of creation came into existence with all of its complex cycles and systems. This is a powerful truth because that same God dwells within us, and He is still speaking. In ourselves we are powerless, but when we speak, the God within us can speak through us to accomplish His work.

I'm sure you have known an insecure person. In fact, I believe we all have experienced insecurity at one time or another. You know—like Al Capp's Joe Btfsplk, the world's worst jinx, walking around with his personal thundercloud overhead. It feels unstable; it feels cold; it feels unsure; it feels *insecure*.

According to Brady Boyd in *Speak Life,* there are three signs of insecurity.

1. You feel inadequate. The most obvious sign of insecurity is feeling inadequate. Do you know someone who is always comparing themselves unfavorably to someone else? They never give themselves any credit for anything!

(a) She sings better than I.
(b) She looks better in that dress than I do.
(c) He has a better job than I.
(d) I could never accomplish what he has.
(e) I'm not as smart as she is.
(f) She seems to always be happy, and I'm not.
(g) He lives in a high-class neighborhood and has a much bigger house than I do.

127

If you constantly compare yourself to others, you will live in a state of depression, feeling less than everyone else. Continuing to do this will get you into deep trouble because your focus is on other people instead of God.

Negative people are looking for you to respond positively to their open-end questions, hoping you will help them feel better about themselves. They say, for example, "I feel fat. Do you think I look fat?" and wait for you to respond, "Oh no! You aren't fat. You look good." *There are never any winners in the comparison game.* The people you compare yourself to have their own customized set of issues. They may have untold dilemmas going on in their life that if you knew about, you would be shocked. But you see only the good side. They look like they have it all together.

What was my comparison game? I would compare myself with other musicians. There was always someone who could play better than I or not as well. I would also compare my speaking abilities with those of others. As always, I never won the game.

Write the areas in which you tend to compare yourself with others.

1. _____

2. _____

3. _____

4. _____

5. _____

6. _____

I felt devastated and inadequate after going through a divorce. Of course by then I was already carrying a full load of garbage. I felt damaged—probably irreparably—and heading for the dump. What man would want a twenty-nine-year-old divorced woman with four little boys under the age of seven? I was miserable until I began believing and then speaking a future into my life. God sent a man who would help me and would someday walk through healing with me. I thank God for my wonderful soulmate and husband.

Even though life comes to a standstill at times, you must begin speaking blessings of future love and grace into your life. Speak to those things that are not as though they were! (See Hebrews 11:1.) Speaking out somehow awakens faith in your heart, and hope springs forth like an oasis in a desert.

2. You feel overlooked. An odd paradox is that even when you're feeling inadequate and whiling away your time playing the comparison game, you sense that your greatness is being overlooked. How can this be? I offer a one-word answer: childishness.

Everybody wants to be acknowledged in some way; nobody likes to be overlooked. We all need words of affirmation, and that's fine, but I'm telling you that we shouldn't go around tooting our own horn so everyone will look our way in admiration. People often do this on social media; they throw themselves out there just in case no one saw their greatness. Proverbs 27:2 says, "Let another man praise you, and not your own mouth; a stranger, and not your own lips."

One year when I was music director at our church, we decided to perform an Easter cantata. As I was assigning solo parts, I felt the hot breath of anger in the air. After a stressful session I was closing down the practice, intending to go home, when a woman asked to speak to me privately. She was jealous and upset because she did not get a solo part! I found myself feeling sorry for this lady, not because she didn't get the part, but because she had no clue this action made her look childish, like a sixth grader who gets upset because she doesn't get picked to be on the volley ball team.

We need to tell ourselves out loud, "God has my life in His hands. He has one person in line for each part or placement or position. God does not make mistakes. If I don't get to play the role I want, I will not gripe and complain that I could do a job better than the person He chose. No, I will choose to wait until He gives me the role He chooses for me. I believe it will be more rewarding and fulfilling than the one I wanted for myself in the first place!"

God has every step of your life in His hands. Even if you make a mistake, if you keep your heart and thinking right, God will take care of it. But if you promote yourself, it will always lead to disaster because it is based upon pride. Say, "God, You have my next move, my next promotion in mind. I give You total liberty to have your way in my life."

Write about the times you thought you were overlooked. How did you feel? How do you plan to deal with it?

1. _____

2. _____

3. _____

4. _____

5. _____

6. _____

   3. *You feel threatened.* Feeling threatened is a classic sign of insecurity. The fact is, whenever insecurity flips our fight-or-flight switch to the "on" position, our personal defense system goes into full alert. Buzzers reverberate, alarms jangle, sirens go whoop-whoop! and we don't know what to do to protect ourselves from the threat.

   I would like to point out that you don't really know what you are capable of. And the funny thing is, the very person who makes you feel insecure may be feeling insecure because of you! You must tell God, "I will go where you want me to go and do my best on the job You want me to do." Not, "God I want to go where that person is going because I can do a better job than they can."

   You might feel threatened by your peers and friends who are being praised for something they did. It might even be in an area in which you have worked so hard. Maybe you accomplished more than this person, but they somehow seemed to get all the recognition for it. You have to learn to tell yourself it's all right, and then praise them for what they have done (and really mean it). Learn to enjoy their accomplishments with them. Don't let negative speech get past your tongue. Sometimes you have to encourage yourself as David did.

   After David slew Goliath, the armies of Israel routed the Philistines and won a great victory. As they were returning from battle, women from every Israelite village and town came out with tambourines and other musical instruments, dancing and singing joyously, "Saul has slain his thousands, and David his ten thousands!" This aroused in Saul the poison of anger, jealousy, and vindictiveness. He thought, *They have ascribed to David ten thousands, and to me only thousands. Now what more can he have but the kingdom?* Verse 9 says, "So Saul eyed David from that day forward." All night long, the poisonous feelings roiled around in his heart and brain, and the next day "a distressing spirit from God came upon Saul." He couldn't handle David stealing his thunder and winning the praise of the people. His pride and anger wouldn't let him acknowledge David's accomplishment; he wanted all the accolades himself.

Brady Boyd, in *Speak Life*, discusses an additional type of threat: insults, persecution, false accusation, and actual threats. The Bible says that when Jesus was reviled, "[He] did not revile in return; when He suffered, He did not threaten, but committed Himself to Him who judges righteously" (I Peter 2:23).

God sees your situation, He cares about your stress, and He is committed to you making it to the other side. When you give God your weakness, He will make you strong. Say out loud, "God is always in control. He sees more than I can see; He sees the big picture. He looks at my heart and spirit, and the hearts of others. God, I give myself to You! And I know I will never be disappointed at the outcome when You are in charge. The outcome will probably be different than I expected, but You can work things out in ways I never would have never thought of! God, everything You do is perfect!"

Do you have some things you need to turn over to God? Write them down.

1. _____

2. _____

3. _____

4. _____

5. _____

Speak life to yourself. Tell yourself you have a future. God is taking all the bad and using it for your good. When you do as He asks, you are going to come out on top. Joy will come in the morning, even though you can't see it in the night. I believe all of this because I have experienced it. I can look back and see the hand of God and what He did in my life. If He did it for me, He will do it for you. Speak life!

Chapter 12

Your Identity: Who You Are in Spirit

Knowing who you are in Christ will make you free. You're probably saying to yourself, "I've heard that a thousand times!" Yes, maybe you have. But has that concept made it to your heart? Or is it still filed away in your head?

As a Borderline I really had to work on this, and I know it is a great struggle for many other people as well. You must plant this knowledge like a seed deep within your spirit until it sprouts, grows, and bears fruit.

When you think of your identity, what comes to mind first?

Following is a list of Scripture passages suggested by Neil Anderson in *Living Free in Christ*. These passages contributed greatly to the success of my healing journey, and I still look them up daily. These Bible passages are the base I work off of, the most valuable tools I have. I not only read them every day, but if at any moment I feel the need, I look one of them up that will help me and read it until my spirit soaks it in like a sponge. Let the Word permeate your mind, heart, soul, and spirit! It will bring truth and rest in the time of need.

Who Am I in Christ?

I am accepted:

John 1:12	I am God's child.
John 15:15	I am Christ's friend.
Romans 5:1	I have been justified.
I Corinthians 6:17	I am one spirit with the Lord.
I Corinthians 6:19–20	I have been bought with a price.
Ephesians 1:1	I am a saint of God.
Ephesians 1:5	I have been adopted as God's child.

133

Ephesians 2:18	I have direct access to God through the Holy Spirit.
Colossians 1:14	I have been redeemed and forgiven.
Colossians 2:10	I am complete in Christ.

I am secure:

Romans 8:1–2	I am free forever from condemnation.
Romans 8:28	God works all things together for my good.
Romans 8:31	I am free from condemnation.
Romans 8:35	I can't be separated from God's love.
II Corinthians 1:21–22	I am established, anointed, and sealed.
Colossians 3:3	I am hidden with Christ in God.
Philippians 1:6	God will keep working in me until I'm perfected.
Philippians 3:20	I am a citizen of heaven.
II Timothy 1:7	I have been given a spirit of love and a sound mind.
Hebrews 4:16	I can find grace and mercy in the time of need.
I John 5:18	I am born of God, and the evil one cannot touch me.

I am significant:

Matthew 5:13–14	I am the salt and light of earth.
John 15:1, 5	I am a branch of the true vine, a channel of His life.
John 15:16	I have been chosen by God and appointed to bear fruit.
Acts 1:8	I am a personal witness of Christ's.
I Corinthians 3:16	I am God's temple.
II Corinthians 5:18–20	I am a minister of reconciliation for God.
II Corinthians 6:1	I am His coworker.
Ephesians 2:6	I am seated with Christ in the heavenly realm.
Ephesians 2:10	I am God's workmanship.

| Ephesians 3:12 | I may approach God with freedom and confidence. |
| Philippians 4:13 | I can do all things through Christ who strengthens me. |

Being aware of and acknowledging your identity in Christ means taking responsibility for who you are. You need to think positively and truthfully. Victorious living does not stem from thinking you're a nobody, or that God doesn't care about you, or that you are doomed to be a failure! You'll never be set free while thinking along those lines.

Use these Scripture verses as you work on taking every thought captive. Place your negative thoughts alongside these verses and see how they measure up. What is the narrative that plays over and over in your mind? After reading these verses, rethink your identity and write it in the space provided below.

_____

_____

Joseph Santoro, in *The Angry Heart,* states, "We are not responsible for how we came to be who we are as adults. But as adults we are responsible for whom we have become and for everything we do and say." Accepting responsibility for your own thinking is not easy. It is so much easier to blame it on your past: "The way I think and feel is *their* fault. All my unhealthy actions are because of what *they* did. After everything they told me, I'll never be able to think anything good about myself."

In taking responsibility for your identity, you must start reading these verses over and over in your mind until you believe them—until they become part of your thinking process. Yes, I still read them every day. I have come to realize how important they are. And yes, I still have insecure moments when I need an emergency dose of reality in Christ, so I go back and reread a verse. I have to take every thought captive and compare it to the Word of God.

Following is a sampling of several verses of Scripture that I use to help me see and realize who I am in Christ.

1. "No longer do I call you servants, for a servant does not know what His master is doing; but I have called you friends, for all things that I heard from My Father I have made known to you" (John 15:15). This verse has been a tremendous help when thinking about God and who He is. When I would have a bad day and was grappling to get control of myself, I would think of God as my friend. How did that help? Well, when you have an issue, who do you go to? Your spouse or family member or lifetime friend. You want to confide in that person who knows you really well and will listen as you pour your heart out.

When I finally let it sink into my heart that God is my best friend, it put things in a whole new perspective. It helped me to feel that God, instead of being a distant, unapproachable being, was right there when I needed Him.

You see, my father shouldered a man-sized responsibility when his mom passed away and my dad, as the oldest child, had to take care of his seven siblings. Then his father, desperate to find work, left home, leaving my thirteen-year-old dad to manage the entire household. Because of this, he never learned a thing about nurturing and providing emotional support; all he knew was *work*. The result was that as a child, I never experienced emotional nurturing from my father.

I believe everyone, to a certain extent, compares their earthly father to the heavenly Father, although they may be unaware of the comparison. I did it, and it was extremely hard for me to fathom that God was close to me, since I wasn't close to my father. I didn't know his heart because he never talked about such things.

Beyond that, there are many people who have been on the receiving end of mental, emotional, or physical abuse by their fathers, making it very difficult for them to have any kind of relationship with God. They look at God as abusive and blame Him for all the bad things that happen around them. They think God is some kind of despotic lord who moves people and things around like serfs trapped in his fiefdom, making sure they are all properly tormented.

Was your dad a perfectionist when you were growing up? Did he demand that everything had to be just right, and there was zero tolerance for mistakes? Did he expect every report card to boast nothing less than straight A's? If so, as an adult you probably feel like

136

you are suspended over the pit of hell by a string. Every time you fail, you expect God will let go of the string and drop you in.

There is a remedy. Jesus said, "I have called you my friend." Plant that seed deep in your heart. Think of everything it implies, and your true identity will break through the soil as a sprout.

2. "But he who is joined to the Lord is one spirit with Him" (I Corinthians 6:17). The NIV renders this verse, "He who unites himself with the Lord is one with him in spirit." Have you ever felt dirty and separated from the Spirit of God? Then this verse is for you. Don't let Satan throw your past in your face, creating a flurry of hopelessness. You are joined to the Lord, and you are one in spirit with Him!

3. "Having predestined us to adoption as sons by Jesus Christ to Himself according to the good pleasure of His will" (Ephesians 1:5). Knowing that I am His child gives me that warm fuzzy feeling that I belong to someone. And that Someone is the King of all kings! My dad had his own business, a very successful tool and die shop. As a child I sometimes visited his shop. Strolling among the work stations and employees, I felt so important and special—I was the owner's daughter! My dad was important, being the business owner, and that meant I was important too.

This is how you must view yourself. You are a child of God! He created the universe, and owns and operates everything on earth. He is very important, and as His child, you are important too. I don't know about you, but that causes the needle on my excitement gauge to serge to the top. No matter if you have taken a wrong turning onto a washed-out road full of ruts and potholes; you can get back on the right road. You can be born into the family of God through repentance, baptism in Jesus' name, and the infilling of the Holy Spirit! Jesus said "whosoever will." That means being born into this wonderful family is possible for everybody who wants it!

4. "For through Him we both have access by one spirit to the Father" (Ephesians 2:18). This verse helped me many times when I wondered if God was even listening to my prayers. It brought joy and peace to my soul knowing that when I needed to talk to Him, He would hear me. I had direct access to Him. I could talk to Him as though He was sitting right beside me.

Be encouraged as you read this: God hears you! He knows your needs and is ready and willing to meet you where you are.

5. "In whom we have redemption through His blood, the forgiveness of sins" (Colossians 1:14). You are not a lost cause. You have not run out of chances. God loves you! He died on the cross so your sins would be forgiven. You mean the world to Him, and He cares passionately about your soul.

Knowing this helped me and still helps me every day. When I would fall short and feel as though I couldn't make it, I would remind myself that my sins were covered with the blood of Jesus. That means He chooses not to remember my mistakes and failures.

6. "And you are complete in Him, who is the head of all principality and power" (Colossians 2:10). Oh did I ever love to know I was complete in Him! As a Borderline, I felt insecure and unsafe a good part of the time, so this verse was my security blanket. Even if I felt myself drifting through space with nowhere to land, I was complete in God. Let this verse speak to you and help you to feel complete in God!

7. "There is therefore now no condemnation to those who do not walk according to the flesh, but according to the Spirit. For the law of the Spirit of life in Christ Jesus has made me free from the law of sin and death" (Romans 8:1–2). These verses were and still are very important to me. Every time I read them I am reminded that as long as I walk "according to the Spirit" no one—not even Satan—can lay any condemnation at my door.

However, if we allow ourselves to dwell on our past mistakes and sins even after we have repented and done everything else we know to do according to God's Word, it sends an invitation for condemnation to creep back into our life and plague our spirit. We must make a conscious effort to remind ourselves that everything we have repented of is under the blood and all is forgiven. As the apostle Paul said, "I forget those things which are behind me."

8. "And we know that all things work together for good to those who love God, to those who are the called according to His purpose" (Romans 8:28). I love this verse! Every time I glance at the

first book I wrote, *Buried Alive*, I think of this verse. No matter how many tangles we have made in the loom of life, if we stop and let Jesus take over, He can weave all of those threads, both the good and the bad, into a beautiful tapestry. He is just in all His ways, and He always keeps His promises.

Some people may look at this verse and think God will not let anything bad happen to them, that His main purpose is to make them comfortable and enjoying the good life. Then they are shocked, disappointed, and angry when their make-believe bubble bursts. Yes, God loves to shower us with good things, but His main goal is not to make us comfortable; it is to make us more like Him! He wants us to live forever with Him in heaven.

9. "Being confident of this very thing, that He who has begun a good work in you will complete it until the day of Jesus Christ" (Philippians 1:6). As long as I allow God to work in me, He will keep working until He comes back to take His bride home. God knows our frame; He knows we are a work in progress. Despite our failures and mistakes, He will never give up on us as long as we let Him keep working. Talk about grace and mercy!

This verse often encouraged me when I fumbled the ball. It let me know that instead of a grandstand full of witnesses booing me, heaven was cheering me on to get up and keep trying. God did and still is doing a wonderful work in me, helping me with my thinking, attitudes, and gifts of the Spirit. He is a faithful God.

10. "For God has not given us a spirit of fear, but of power and of love and of a sound mind" (II Timothy 1:7). Many times I would walk into my office stricken with fear and thinking that nothing I did made a lick of sense. I would sit down and quote this verse over and over. I knew if I was fearful, it was not God. God is not about fear; He is about love. In times past I allowed fear to grip my heart until I was immobilized. In that state I made some awful decisions and said some awful things. Yet now, when I read this verse, I feel God's arms come around me and hear His still small voice saying, "Everything is going to be all right."

I encourage you to use this verse often. God is love and security. He will move in and replace fear with love. God is a sure foundation on which to stand in the time of trouble.

11. "Let us therefore come boldly to the throne of grace, that we may obtain mercy and find grace to help in the time of need" (Hebrews 4:16). God has a storehouse of unlimited mercy and grace! I needed this verse many times when I was running on empty. Repeating it often and hiding it in my heart taught me much about grace and mercy during my healing journey. We tend to put limits on God, but God has no limits! His hands are extended out to us. There: see the nail prints? If Jesus died for you, there's nothing He won't do for you so you can make it to heaven.

Don't ever feel like you've done something that God's mercy and grace cannot cover. On one of our evangelistic trips, we came across a man in an inner-city church that was studying for his ministerial license. We were surprised to learn he had been on death row three times, sentenced to die in the electric chair because he had murdered seven people. Yet God thought he was worth saving, and, after cleaning up his life, thought he was worthy to be used of God in ministry. I know many more people to whom God has extended His grace and mercy and now they are living a victorious life because of it. You also can live an abundant life through Christ.

12. "You did not choose Me, but I chose you and appointed you that you should go and bear fruit, and that your fruit should remain, that whatever you ask the Father in My name He may give you" (John 15:16). This verse always made me feel wonderful deep down inside to know that God chose me! Those times when I felt I had slipped so far behind that I would never gain the ground I had lost, this verse strengthened me. The cycling characteristic of BPD brought those thoughts and feelings periodically, and at those times I needed to know the King of kings still chose me when I felt less than my best.

I still remember the feeling I had back in my school days, because I always seemed to be one of the last ones picked for the softball, kickball, or soccer team. I hated that constant feeling of rejection. I felt all eyes were on me and my flaws were under the scrutiny of everyone on the ball field.

Just imagine standing in a line and having God choose you. That's exactly what happens: He chooses each one of us! I get excited when I think about being chosen by Him. He makes me feel as though I am worth having on His team. I am His disciple, one of the called people. I was placed in the royal priesthood. I am a child of the King, and so are you!

When you feel rejected, just remember you are one of the chosen! God didn't take the team onto the playing field and leave you standing in line for the devil to snatch for his team. God picked you first!

13. "Do you not know that you are the temple of God and that the Spirit of God dwells in you?" (I Corinthians 3:16). It is heaven to know that in spite of my shortcomings I am the temple of God. God dwells in my heart. Knowing this is like a breath of fresh air to my soul. Wherever I am, God is there too. Be encouraged today; you are the temple of God. He dwells in you. You don't have to be perfect or flawless, because greater is He that is in you than He that is in the world!

14. "For we are His workmanship, created in Christ Jesus for good works, which God prepared beforehand that we should walk in them" (Ephesians 2:10). Think about it: the God of heaven prepared our steps before we were even born. That's incredible! We are important to God. I cherish the time I spend in my prayer closet when God assures me that He knows me and how I operate. He made me; I am His workmanship.

You are God's workmanship! He prepared your steps before you were born. He does not leave you to walk alone or decide which pathway to take. He has it all mapped out for you and He will lead you. All you have to do is follow in His steps. You are His workmanship!

15. "In whom we have boldness and access with confidence through faith in Him" (Ephesians 3:12). Yes, I can enter into the heavenly realm with boldness and confidence, believing He is going to hear me. I knew this before my healing journey, but it became more real along the way. I learned God always hears me, and just because He does not answer right away doesn't mean He will never answer. I believe if God gave us immediate answers every time we asked, we wouldn't appreciate it properly; our faith and spiritual growth would be stunted. May I remind you from my own experience that God

doesn't usually come through according to our schedule? His timing is always different than ours—but it is always perfect.

Don't be discouraged when you go boldly before God and yet you don't receive what you expected. Give Him time to work. Keep the faith and keep your head held high. God loves you and invites you to approach Him anytime you need to. He is your heavenly Father and He loves you with an everlasting love. He has a storehouse of good things to give you, but He knows the best time to bestow them. We don't.

16. "I can do all things through Christ who strengthens me" (Philippians 4:13). This was and still is my most-quoted verse. This verse is incredibly encouraging and uplifting! It lets me know I can do anything with His help and strength; there are no limits. It doesn't matter what I am going through, where I have been, or where my road might lead me, I can do all things through Christ. At my weakest hour, I can speak out through tears of desperation and fear, "God, I can do all things through You! I can do this! Yes I can!"

You too can pray that prayer. Don't let the devil tell you that you are a failure and a nobody. You are a child of God! As your Father, He walks by your side, helping you accomplish things you never dreamed you could do. God always comes through.

After reading these Scripture passages and recognizing who you are in Christ, how do you feel?

_____

_____

What stands out to you the most?

_____

_____

In what area do you feel like you are lacking the most?

_____

I encourage you to know and work on your identity in Christ. I have offered material in this chapter that you can use on a daily basis. These verses will strengthen your spirit. You can walk confidently, knowing your true identity in Christ. Then your life will be abundant, joyful, and full of glory.

Chapter 13

Your Identity: Who You Are in Flesh

I believe one of the things people struggle with a great deal is body image. I would be safe in saying it's more of a female issue than a male's, but some men suffer from it as well. We often let our physical appearance determine our self-worth. For instance, some have suffered from obesity all of their life. Children can be brutally honest and at times hurtful and not even realize they have hurt another child, possibly scarring them for life.

There once was a girl I'll call Wilma who was always a little on the chubby side. One day as she was having fun playing with her friends down the street, a girl named Sara told her, "You're fat!" It wasn't true, but it upset Wilma. From then on she assumed everyone viewed her as fat and didn't want anything to do with her.

This happens to more people than you would think. They try to bury the hurt and move on, but it's hard. These incidents affect every other part of their life, even their relationships, and many times they do not realize it.

Nancy Leigh DeMoss, in *Lies Women Believe*, lists several of the lies individuals will tell themselves:

1. I'll always be fat.
2. Nobody could ever like me or want me to be their friend.
3. I'm worthless.
4. I have to be the life of the party in order to be liked or accepted by others.

"Esther" was a lady I once knew who, at the age of eighty-three, was still struggling with body image. When she was a little girl, her mother woke her up each morning with the words, "Come on and get your fat, slobby self out of bed!" As long as I knew Esther, she was never what I would consider big. Granted, a few times in her life she carried an extra twenty pounds, but never was obese. Yet she grew up thinking she was fat.

Her mother wasn't the only one contributing to the problem. As a child, sometimes when Esther was lagging behind her friends who were running down the street, they would turn around and yell, "Whatsa matter fatty? Can't you run?" She dieted all of her life, always keeping track of the calories she was consuming. Going to the store was a chore as she slowly worked her way down the aisles reading the labels on each food item she picked up. She would step on the scale every day, hoping she had not gained even a tenth of a pound. The stress of all this weighed her down daily. She suffered from gastric issues, all because she could not see herself objectively and control what she thought about her body.

There are many out there just like Esther. All too often they identify with what people think about their outward appearance. Their memories hark back to that popular girl or guy back in grade school they wanted so much to be like, or to the homecoming queen in high school, thinking, *Wow, she was so beautiful!*

I was blessed not to have a weight problem, but I still struggled with body image. A person does not have to be overweight to feel unsatisfied with their body. Back when I was a teenager I imagined I had a big stomach, so I wore undergarments to hold it in. Ironically, I was always under my ideal weight.

Let's stop here a moment. I want you to think about how you feel about your body image. Are you satisfied with it for the most part?

_____

_____

If the answer is no, what are the things you wish to change about your body in order to be happy with it?

1. _____

2. _____

3. _____

4. _____

Low self-esteem is one of the most common diagnoses today, and I suspect the root of the problem is body image. Several years ago while my husband was serving as youth pastor, he conducted a short survey of his students. He asked them to write down something they did not like about themselves. After collecting their answers, he discovered every one of them had written something they didn't like about their body. In addition, the things they were unsatisfied with could not be changed. Sadly, most people are unsatisfied with the way they look. If only they could learn to love themselves, they would be so much happier. Below is an acrostic from Nancy DeMoss's book:

Love Yourself

Let go of the "shoulds" in your life.
Open up to the miracle of you.
Value your uniqueness.
Explore your dreams and passions.

Yield to life—go with the flow.
Obey the voice of your spirit.
Unwind—get cozy and comfy.
Renew yourself—body and soul.
Surround yourself with caring people.
Express yourself—be true to you.
Linger longer at what you enjoy.
Feel God's special love for you.

We were created in the image of God. Genesis 1:27 says, "So God created man in His own image, in the image of God created he him; male and female created he them." God created you in His own image. There is no better image to be created by than Jesus Christ! How do you think God feels when His children are disappointed with their looks?

In Psalm 139:14–16 (KJV) David exulted, "I will praise thee; for I am fearfully and wonderfully made: marvellous are thy works; and that my soul knoweth right well. My substance was not hid from thee, when I was made in secret, and curiously wrought in the lowest parts of the earth. Thine eyes did see my substance, yet being imperfect; and in thy book all my members were written, which in continuance were fashioned, when as yet there was none of them."

God not only created you in His image, but He was responsible for creating every part of your body. God does not make mistakes. He knows what He is doing. Yes, some people are born with birth defects, some caused by the choices their mothers made during pregnancy, some designed by God. But there is a reason and purpose for everything He does. God decides how tall you will be, whether you will be male or female, and the kind of build you will have—stocky or slender. He decides what color your hair will be, the shape of your nose, face, and ears, and what color your beautiful eyes will be. God designed you! No matter how much science tampers with human genomes and embryos, no one can ever take the place of God and His creation.

Some surgeons are getting rich by operating on people who are desperate to change their body image. Some patients have so many surgeries that they look like a different person. Some even take it to the extreme and have a sex-change operation. Can you imagine how God feels? This type of behavior, in my opinion, is a shame, and it dishonors God.

Homosexuality

There has been an ongoing debate on whether homosexuality is "born or bred." Supporters from the medical field as well as the media have pointed to an article based on UCLA research and published in October 2003 by the journal *Molecular Brain Research*. The research indicated that sexual identity is genetic. Reuters picked up the story, claiming that since "sexual identity is wired into the genes," the research proved that homosexuality and transgender sexuality are determined genetically. Soon this interpretation was all over the media, touted as one more piece of evidence for a genetic theory of homosexuality.

However, Princeton Professor Dr. Jeffrey Satinover, MD, rightly commented on the UCLA research: "The hormonal milieu that causes sexual differentiation between males and females is itself determined by genes. . . . This comes as no surprise. But this research says absolutely nothing about homosexuality or transsexualism and any who claim it does are either ill-informed about genetics, or if not, are deliberately abusing their scientific knowledge and or credentials in the service of politics" (stated in an email dated October 21, 2003.

In effect, Satinover was saying, somewhat facetiously, "Of course a baby's sex is determined by 'hormonal milieu' as the child develops. Duh, everybody on both sides of the argument knows that. But don't try to jump to any other conclusions beyond what the research shows. You politically correct people can't say the research proves that homosexuality is in the genes. It says nothing of the kind, and if you are honest you will admit that."

Robert Knight, director of the Culture and Family Institute, commented further, "Americans for too long have been pummeled with the idea that people are 'born gay.' The people who most need to hear the truth are those who mistakenly believe they have no chance themselves for change. *It is both more compassionate and truthful to give them hope* than to serve them up politically motivated, unproven creations like the 'gay gene'" (from Knight's article "Born or Bred," https://concernedwomen.org/images/content/bornorbred.pdf, emphasis mine).

As we have seen, "God created man in His own image . . . male and female He created them." He designed it this way to propagate the earth and to form the family as the basis of society. God clearly views homosexuality as a deviant behavior: "You shall not lie with a male as with a woman. It is an abomination. . . . If a man lies with a male as he lies with a woman, both of them have committed an abomination. They shall surely be put to death. Their blood shall be upon them" (Leviticus 18:22; 20:13).

Yet there is hope because God is a healer and a deliver! In I Corinthians 6:11, Paul said of the former homosexuals who had become believers, "Such were some of you. But you were washed, but you were sanctified, but you were justified in the name of the Lord Jesus and by the Spirit of our God."

Personally, I view the sin of same-sex attraction like any other sin people struggle with. This gives me a better understanding of where they might be coming from. Yes, same-sex behavior is deadly wrong if acted upon just like a person who acts upon their drug addiction or alcoholism, kleptomania or pornography. It's all wrong and should be brought under control with prayer, fasting, spiritual disciplines, and many times, counseling. The battle is real. We have a

149

tendency to shy away from people who struggle in this area. Sometimes the tendency for same-sex attraction stems from past abuse or unhealthy relationships, but God can deliver and heal any human condition. God loves us all and is faithful to forgive, restore, and help all to come to a healthy self-esteem and true understanding of our identity.

Some people suffer with eating disorders, such as anorexia and bulimia. Below are two articles from The Soul Care Bible:

Bulimia Nervosa

People who have bulimia consume large amounts of food in a short period of time (bingeing), then feel out of control and unable to stop eating. Bingeing is often followed by various methods to expel the food from the body—vomiting, diuretics, laxatives, or excessive exercise. While their bodies are usually normal in size, people with bulimia often base their self-worth on their weight and shape, feeling that they must be thinner.

The exact cause of bulimia is unknown. Culture and glamorized norms certainly contribute. Bulimia can be impacted by stress or be a response to trauma. In most cases, bulimia begins during high school or college. Some common warning signs include: secretive behavior coupled with trips to the bathroom after eating, laxative or diuretic abuse, heart palpitations, depression, social withdrawal, restrictive dieting, frequent and obvious weight fluctuations, and a preoccupation with body weight and appearance.

There are many reasons why bulimia is serious, including the possibility of esophageal tears, gastric ruptures, and dehydration. In addition, psychological, social, and emotional damage are often experienced by those struggling with bulimia.

Anorexia

Anorexia involves a pattern with not eating enough. Those affected by it are in a battle for control. If they cannot control other parts of their lives, they will control their food intake. People with anorexia refuse to keep their body weight at a normal level because they are unable to accurately view the shape and size of their own body. They may be very thin, but still think they are fat. They continue to try to lose weight through a much lower food intake, often coupled with extreme amounts of exercise. Similar to bulimia, their body weight affects their self-esteem.

The daily grind of those who experience anorexia is exhausting. . . . Much time is spent on the scale and in front of the mirror. On top of that, hours can be spent exercising. Essentially, people who suffer with this disease are starving themselves to death. The underlying futile attempt at perfection lurks continuously. This attempt is fueled by several fears: fear of fat, fear of failure, fear of being less than perfect, fear of rejection, or fear of losing control.

People who struggle with these disorders suffer silently every day. It's really hard for other people to work with them whether it be a family member or friend. Remember the struggle is real. I have heard that an eating disorder is one of the hardest disorders to conquer, but nonetheless, it is not too hard for God.

During my young adult years I had a friend who suffered with bulimia. I took her to the emergency room on several occasions because of dehydration. She had been sexually and mentally abused by a family member when she was quite young, and it had left many lasting effects upon her life. She finally went into an intensive rehab center and with the help of therapy and God, she was able to overcome the disorder. This is another true miracle. She has a great future and is currently doing a wonderful work for the Lord.

Just as first aid cannot cure cancer, a Band-Aid cannot cure these eating disorders. A person's psychological and spiritual past must be delved into to find out what is driving the disorder. The steps of healing in this book will help, along with a counselor who specializes in this area. He or she will be able to determine the exact treatment you need.

Do you suffer with same-sex attraction or an eating disorder? Yes or No

If you do, what are your thoughts and feelings about it? What is screaming inside of you that you wish you could say and someone would understand?

1. _____

2. _____

3. _____

4. _____

5. _____

6. _____

"How precious also are Your thoughts to me, O God! How great is the sum of them! If I should count them, they would be more in number than the sand: when I awake, I am still with You" (Psalm 139:17–18).

God not only knows all of your thoughts, but He has many precious thoughts of you! Have you ever gone to the beach, scooped up a handful of sand, and tried to count how many grains of sand you were holding? Probably not, because it would be impossible. I believe these verses are saying God's wonderful thoughts about you began at the moment of conception and will go on forever. How precious is that?

Through prayer, the Word of God, counseling, and the steps outlined in this book, God helped me to accept and embrace my body that God created. None of us have perfect bodies and never will, but God made us just as He wanted us to be.

Are you feeling any better about your body image? Yes or No

Write down some positive things about your body that you are starting to see. Go ahead; look at yourself through the eyes of Jesus!

1. _____

2. _____

3. _____

4. _____

5. _____

6. _____

Great! You can love yourself—because you are beautiful in God's eyes! I remember the day I came to the sudden realization that I was no longer worrying about my weight and how I looked. I was okay with myself. What freedom I felt! What a peace of mind knowing that God created me, body, soul, and spirit.

Embrace how your God created you so skillfully. You are beautiful inside and out. God has helped you to have a healthy view of what your identity is in flesh. Let your new positive feelings about yourself come bursting outward in your speech and worshipful response to your Creator!

Chapter 14

Grounding and Focusing

God has to be the focus of every grounding exercise; this involves meditating on all His work and wonders and depending on His strength. This is vitally important in your healing journey. If you don't include God, it is impossible to be completely healed! Many psychiatric centers do not incorporate a biblical experience, with the result that many of their patients will relapse time and time again. The prescription for complete healing is brokenness, repentance, forgiveness, and restitution along with prayer and the Word of God. God must be the center of everything we say, do, and think.

People often get a little spooked when they hear words like *grounding, focusing, meditation.* These words are not to be feared or questioned; they are great tools when used at the right time, in the right form, in a positive way. Remember we are body, soul, and spirit, and we must have different tools to maintain the health of each of these components. Just as the proper amount and quality of food helps our bodies survive and thrive, I have learned certain exercises that will keep our minds focused and grounded where they need to be.

> *I will also meditate on all Your work, and talk of Your deeds. Your way, O God, is in the sanctuary; who is so great a God as our God? You are the God who does wonders; You have declared Your strength among the peoples. (Psalm 77:12–14)*

We must be sure we are using tools that please God. This is one reason why it's very important to have an apostolic, Spirit-filled counselor who will not lead you astray. As I have said before, I had a fabulous counselor in Vani Marshall. I felt safe in her capable hands, and we had many God moments that led to my complete miracle healing. If you don't have a counselor and need one, Vani Marshall is the one for you!

Dan B. Allender, in *The Wounded Heart,* explains, "When an abused person feels powerless, she internalizes an image of herself as profoundly inadequate. She deeply questions her ability, competence, and intelligence. Failure at a task seems to imply inability, incompetence, or lack of motivation. The abused woman will often see herself as mentally deficient."

Many people can relate to the above statements. When this happened to me, I felt the need to go to a safe, quiet room all by myself to do some grounding and focusing. When I say "safe place," I don't mean that other places in my home were not safe. I did, however, need a certain place in my house that was quiet and peaceful—a room where I would not be interrupted while doing grounding exercises—a place where God and I could meet.

When is the proper time to do grounding and focusing? Most of the time, it will be very apparent to you. Your support person can also help you in this area. Here are some of the indications that let me know I needed grounding:

1. A feeling of confusion
2. Lack of concentration
3. A feeling of hopelessness
4. A feeling of rejection
5. Inability to form words
6. Inability to hold a constructive conversation
7. Crying with no apparent reason
8. Inability to make a decision
9. Lack of control
10. Having a hard time taking every thought captive
11. Wanting to run away from everything

Here is a sample of some more serious indications people may have to deal with:

1. Wanting to run to your addiction (drugs, alcohol, gambling, eating, etc.)
2. Cutting or harming yourself
3. Thoughts of suicide
4. Wanting to be destructive or harmful to someone
5. Wanting to destroy property
6. Feelings of anger
7. Feelings of fear

8. Feelings of failure
9. Depression
10. Unexplained anxiety

Can you identify with some of the above feelings and situations? Which ones? List them below.

1. _____

2. _____

3. _____

4. _____

5. _____

6. _____

Are there are some circumstances/situations not listed here that would apply to you?

1. _____

2. _____

3. _____

4. _____

5. _____

6. _____

There are many types of grounding, and you must pick and choose which ones you believe will be the most beneficial to you. Try to be patient and go easy on yourself. I struggled with being too hard on myself at times. It caused a lot of unneeded anxiety. Don't except an instant miracle. Sometimes you will find more than one grounding exercise will help you. Sometimes you must either repeat the same exercise or do a variety of exercises to get your mind and spirit grounded and back to where it needs to be. You will reap great benefits from these exercises if you are faithful to them. For example, I found that the closer I got to my total healing the less time it took for me to get grounded again. It does get easier as time goes on.

Remember the journey toward your miracle healing, just like other aspects of life, is a process with many ups and downs, good days and bad days. For example, if you are dieting, you will have easy days when you eat all the right things and exercise properly; but other days, you blow it. Then you want to give up . . . but you don't.

That's the key: don't give up! You will fail at times and not get the result you want, but get up, dust yourself off, and start again. The important part is getting back up. Micah 7:8 says, "Do not rejoice over me, my enemy; when I fall, I will arise; when I sit in darkness, the LORD will be a light to me."

This verse says, *when* I fall, not *if* I fall. We try hard not to fall, but we are human and still grappling with our carnal, sinful nature. Every word and deed is not perfect—we do not have glorified bodies yet. Thus we must carry on with the mindset that we are going to fall, but when it happens we must already know and be determined that we will get back up again. This is very important! You should always have a get-back-up plan. This is where your support group can be of vital help to you. Sometimes it takes one of your supporters to look you in the face and tell you, "Get back up! You can do this! I believe in you! You can do anything through Christ who strengthens you!"

In order for this to happen, you have to reach out. You have to let that person know that you need their help, or maybe you need to call your counselor. Whatever it may be, you can do it. There must always be some action taken when you cannot get back up on your own.

Joseph Santoro, in *The Angry Heart,* offers some grounding techniques that were very helpful to me throughout my healing process. They may take some practice, but once the technique is mastered, I'm convinced they will help you too.

The Slow Deep Breathing Routine

A. Find a quiet place where you will not be interrupted for about fifteen minutes. (I always turned off my phone and dimmed the lights, which seemed to have a calming effect.) Rate your stress level on a 0–10 scale where 0 means totally calm and stress-free and 10 means totally stressed out.

Pre-Practice Relaxation Rating

0	1	2	3	4	5	6	7	8	9	10
Total Calm								Total Stress		

B. Sit in a comfortable chair with your feet flat on the floor. Place your hands palms-down on or near your knees.

C. Close your eyes and listen to all of the sounds in your environment for a few moments. Try to focus your thoughts on what you hear. If your thoughts wander, gently squeeze your knees and return your attention to a sound. (For me, this was hard to do at times when my mind was full of racing thoughts, but it is possible to do. Keep with it; you can do it!)

D. After a minute or two begin slow deep breathing (SDB). Breathe in through your nose while counting from 1–10. Try to make your inhale last until you reach ten. Try to fill your lower abdominal area with air first, then your midsection, and finally your chest. Try to expand your lungs as much as possible. It may make you feel uncomfortable at first; however, with a little practice your ability to expand your lungs will increase.

E. After you have fully inhaled, hold your breath for a count of 3.

F. Then exhale slowly and count backwards from 10–1. As you exhale, think *I am calm* over and over again. Try to see these words light up in your mind as clearly as you can.

G. Repeat the SDB cycle for about ten to fifteen minutes or until you feel noticeably calmer. Once you get into an SDB rhythm, you can stop counting and just breathe. (If you are a mother, you will see this step is quite similar to focus-breathing during labor. I feel that SDB, along with relaxation and focusing, truly helps to reduce pain.)

H. After you feel calmer, open your eyes and rate your stress level again. How much calmer do you feel? A post-practice rating of 3 or less on the 0–10 relaxation scale is your goal.

Post-Practice Relaxation Rating

0	1	2	3	4	5	6	7	8	9	10
Total Calm								Total Stress		

God gave us a powerful mind. If we can learn how to use it to our advantage, it will help us greatly. We need to learn to use what God gave us. He created us with a will of our own and gave us freedom to make our own choices. Therefore we can't expect God to do it all; we must do our part. Learning to reprogram our unhealthy thinking is part of letting God transform our mind. We have to create new inroads before we can achieve a new way of thinking.

When you start thinking differently, having better reactions, making better choices, and exhibiting a better demeanor, you will know you are well on your way to healing. Don't get me wrong—getting this far is a lot of work, but with God all things are possible!

Santoro continues the discussion by describing the art of objectifying:

Objectifying

Objectifying is a skill that empowers a person to look at a situation, and the emotions, thoughts, and

160

impulses that go with it, with full awareness and choice. Objectifying is the opposite of impulsive reaction or gratification. It is a soothing skill because, like SDB, it will help keep you calm and safe.

Your objective is to focus your awareness on the stressful situation, and the emotions, thoughts, and impulses that go with it, while describing what is happening to you, what you are feeling, and what you are thinking, as a TV reporter might do. That is, describe it as if you were observing everything from the outside. Your job is to report everything without reacting. Remember, objectifying means describing what is happening without reacting to it.

This skill is harder to develop than SDB . . . because of your psych traumatic experiences (your instinct is to numb, deny, forget, or stuff stressful feelings). This skill . . . will help prevent you from impulsively reacting in a self-injurious way to stressors.

In my healing journey, I discovered I was already "objectifying" before I read about it in *The Angry Heart*. This discovery was another God-moment when I saw how God was leading me and teaching me to make a new road, a new pathway in my thinking process. It gives me great excitement to think and write about this because those were key moments in my healing.

You see, my healing journey progressed in three phases, the first being to see and understand why my thinking was incorrect. Here is a hypothetical example to explain what I mean:

My friend Cynthia says, "Oh, I bet you had to really hurry through the preparations in order to get this all done!" She means, "You did a really great job! With your busy schedule I imagine you really had to hurry to pull this off. A lot of people wouldn't have been able to do it!" But my take is, "Cynthia thinks I did a rush job. She thinks I didn't plan ahead and therefore didn't pace myself. She's dropping a hint that I need to do a better job next time!"

This is how I processed as a Borderline. As I began to heal, I recognized my thinking process was inaccurate; I was misconstruing the meaning of other people's statements. You see a Borderline is all about themselves. They only think about how the statement affects them, and they see it with a negative slant. It is their world and their world only. So it was a milestone when I began to recognize and understand what people actually meant when they spoke to me.

The second phase of my healing was saying out loud the correct interpretation of Cynthia's statement: "She is giving me a compliment, saying that although I have a busy schedule I was still able to pull off the finished project with excellence." Articulating this helped my mind to understand, but my emotions were still programmed to react as if her comment was an insult. Cynthia could still feel the wall go up between us because my emotions had not switched over to the new way of thinking. Thus the third and final phase was to correctly interpret Cynthia's statement and have the appropriate emotional response.

Be patient with yourself because you often will take three steps forward and two steps backward. You will feel defeated, but pull yourself back up and go on where you left off. Understand that you have been thinking incorrectly anywhere from twenty to forty years or more, so healing and reprogramming and transforming your mind will take time. But it will happen. God is faithful and just. He always comes through!

Now that you have read my example of wrong thinking, can you recall some conversations that you might have misconstrued? If so, write them in the space provided below:

1. _____

2. _____

3. _____

4. _____

5. _____

I want you to take some time and think about what you wrote. You may not have BPD, but this kind of thinking is characteristic of all unhealthy thinking.

Borderlines do not base their responses or conclusions on facts; it's all about emotions—and emotions can be tricky. What happens when a Borderline's response comes from emotion only? They come up with a different answer every time. They are inconsistent; they flip back and forth with each passing feeling. There is no structure on which to base their response or opinion. This can be very frustrating for family and friends, because the Borderline agrees with them one minute and the next will be upset with them and turn totally against them because their emotions have flipped to the other side of the issue. This is where the term *Borderline* comes from. It denotes bouncing from one side to the other without knowing what one really believes.

I'm not saying that emotions should not factor in when we listen and respond to someone, but we must always respond appropriately to the true meaning of the other person's statements.

Next, Santoro describes the art of visualizing:

Visualizing

When visualizing, you use your imagination to create a powerful motivating image in your mind's eye. Imagination is an ability that everyone has, though few of us make full use of its enormous potential. Many people, however use their imagination to think up all the horrible things that could happen. They catastrophize about what could happen and in doing so conjure all of the negative emotions that accompany the imaginary disasters.

Using Visualization, you can harness the power of your imagination to guide yourself toward well-thought-out actions that keep you safe and improve the quality of your life.

Your objective is to visualize yourself engaged in positive action scenes in place of self-destructive, impulsive reactions to stressors. A well-visualized scene acts as a model for your behavior to follow. It motivates you to

163

match your behavior to that model. It also helps you to confront your tendency toward negative thinking. Negative thinking leads you to expect the worse, even though you may say otherwise to yourself and others. . . .
The more you use visualization the less impulsive and unpredictable your actions will become.

The Basic Steps of Visualization

1. Close your eyes.
2. Begin your SDB routine. Continue until your stress level drops below 4 on your [relaxation] scale.
3. Now imagine yourself executing a series of actions that produces a desirable outcome. Imagine as much detail as possible. See yourself doing the actions. See where you are. See who you are with. Here the sounds. Smell the odors. See what you are wearing.
4. As negative thoughts enter your mind, squeeze your knees, and return to your visualization.
5. Once you have imagined all of the details of your action sequence, keep that positive picture in your mind so that you can [easily] recall it when you need to.

These visualization steps may sound a little odd to you, but I assure you it's not a mind-over-matter technique or anything "way out there." It is just a simple exercise to help you get hold of your thoughts and become a more consistent person. You have allowed your mind to wander to negative places for so long that you must learn to control and retrain your thought process until you can think positively.

It will help to incorporate the Word of God into these steps. When you see yourself doing something positive, think about "seeing those things that are not as though they were!" Imagine yourself receiving your miracle healing. Think about that lost loved one receiving the gift of the Holy Ghost. Picture yourself as healed and whole and serving God with joy.

The goal is to get complete control of your mind and create channels that guide your thoughts along positive lines. You no longer will let your thoughts wander to the point you dissociate and become insecure. Your emotions will not run amok and your thoughts to places they should not go.

> Finally, brethren, whatever things are true, whatever things are noble, whatever things are just, whatever things are pure, whatever things are lovely, whatever things are of good report, if there is any virtue and if there is anything praiseworthy—meditate on these things. The things which you learned and received and heard and saw in me, these do and the God of peace will be with you. (Philippians 4:8–9)

You will have peace when you think on these things! Incorporate them into your exercises. Objectifying and visualizing will help you calm down, focus, and regain control of your mind so you can think straight, think positive, and achieve mental health. Make an accurate mental assessment of what has been said, articulate it, visualize yourself completing a positive task and doing something good, then bask in the peace God will bring to your mind and heart.

Santoro recommends giving yourself positive affirmation twice every day, once in the morning and once in the evening just before bedtime. I go a step further. I think it's good to come up with six sentences of affirmation you would like to hear someone tell you every day. Repeat those affirmations to yourself two times a day. Here is an example of my affirmations:

1. I am not to blame for having BPD.
2. I am responsible for changing my thinking and behavior.
3. I want to change and I can do this.
4. I am a good person.
5. I have several really good qualities and talents.
6. I will never give up until I receive my complete healing.

After reading the above list, construct your own affirmation sentences to minister to your individual needs:

1. _____

2. _____

3. _____

4. _____

5. _____

6. _____

"Affirmation helps you to construct a better mental image of yourself and your behavior," says Joseph Santoro in *The Angry Heart*. He goes on to say:

> Use decisions to build your lifestyle in the same way a mason uses bricks to build a house. A solid lifestyle rests on a foundation of solid decisions. Decisions select your environments. They give you access to situations that in turn influence your behavior. Bad decisions can haunt you, and good decisions can delight you. Some decisions can affect your life for years to come.

I can relate to this. At times I have made some really good decisions that delighted me. But I've also made some haunting split-second decisions that were devastating. Some of them probably will never be fixed. All I can do is place the consequences in God's hands. My husband used to say, "Never make a decision, good or bad, when you are at a high or a low emotionally in your life." That is very good advice. We usually make poor decisions during those times. For instance, if you are on an emotional high, you have a tendency to bite off more than you can chew. You think you can conquer the world. Then, when everything falls through, you plunge into an emotional low.

I want to encourage you to try these exercises suggested by Joseph Santoro. I would not have mentioned them if they hadn't help me. Besides the exercises mentioned in this chapter, I have practiced everything recommended in Santoro's book and reaped great benefits.

Remember I believe in you because I believe in God. With God's help and your own efforts, you can become that person God created you to be!

Chapter 15

Tracking Your Progress

Everyone's track record will look different because each individual has various emotional problems, personality disorders, and challenges. I'm sure many have used the steps of healing mentioned in this book for a wide variety of reasons. I believe these steps of healing will work in all types of situations; however, some people require a great deal of counseling, and/or medication, and a support team. Some have addictions that might require an inpatient or outpatient detox program. The point is many variables come into play when one is tracking one's progress.

I will say there is no right or wrong time for anyone's healing. I always use the word "process" because that is exactly what it is. If you're on the road to healing, I feel you are doing fine as long as you are moving forward. However, when you come to a standstill, it's okay as long as you are *putting forth the effort* to move forward. I say this because you most likely will hit a rough spot in the road or be halted by a barrier. You feel as though you will never reach the journey's end. Just hold on. You can work to smooth out the rough spots and take down the barriers. Progress may be so slow and gradual that you hardly notice the changes until you take the time to look back and reflect on how far you've come. At some point, something will happen and you will be surprised that your reaction is different than what it used to be. You will say, "Wow, did you see that? I never used to be able to respond so well in this type of situation. This is God's healing power in action!"

Here is a practical example to illustrate my point: You take your car to the automatic carwash and carefully maneuver it onto the conveyor belts. At some point you are instructed to put your car in neutral. Your take your foot off the gas pedal and your hands off the steering wheel. You're doing nothing to make the car move, but it's still moving easily and smoothly, albeit slowly, down the track.

When you're in "neutral," God is saying to you, "Be still and know that I am God" as He takes the wheel and maneuvers you into new territory. All you have to do is go with the flow until He has moved you to the place He wants. When you reach the other side, God says, "Now put your car in gear, take the wheel, and go!" As you start driving, you are amazed. "Wow! What just happened? Something is different. I feel like a new person. I am cleaner and shinier than when I pulled into this carwash!" You then realize God did what He does best: while you were resting, He did all the driving while at the same time "operating" on your mind!

These God-moments are instantaneous and indescribable. Moments like these happened to me many times along my healing journey. For instance, my husband and I started evangelizing about the same time I started my healing journey. Sometimes after a revival service I didn't know exactly what God had done for me (or to me) or what part of my mind He had healed; I just knew I felt different inside. As we would go on with our schedule, it wouldn't be long until I began to notice the differences in my thinking process and responses. I remember times in Vani's office as I lay on the floor before God while He saturated me with His power and performed surgery on my heart. God knows just what we need and when we need it. His timing is perfect!

When my journey seemed long and hot and dusty, I wished God would just instantaneously heal me. "Please, God, do it right now!" However, He was merciful and did not answer that prayer. I don't think I would have been able to handle an instantaneous transformation. The shock would have floored me. I just kept plodding along, making slow progress until I came to a point when I had to stop and ask myself, "Who am I?" It was as if I had started a new life, like I had these before-and-after pictures. I had been reborn. I would look back at things I said and the way I had responded to certain situations and people's comments, and it was like looking back at a different person. It took quite a while to get through that phase of my healing.

People who have cancer often have to take chemotherapy drugs and may experience a wide variety of phenomena: "metal mouth" (food doesn't taste the same), "chemo-brain" (loss of short-term memory, inability to concentrate on reading, etc.) nausea, insomnia, joint pain, fatigue, weakness, tingling in the extremities. And all of a sudden they have no hair!

Our youngest son, Austin, was diagnosed with Hodgkin's Lymphoma at the age of three and underwent chemotherapy and radiation. It totally changed his life and routine. He became a different little boy for a while. After the series of treatments ended, Austin had to go through some physical therapy in order to strengthen his muscles. The strong medicines had totally changed his little body. Austin is now a strong, healthy young man, but he traversed a long, slow journey to recovery.

I'm telling you these things so you won't expect to skip through the adjustments you have to make along the way. Progress at times will be painstakingly slow. But God is faithful and just. He does all things for your good!

Self-Awareness and Honesty

As I said earlier in this book, honesty was a hurdle for me. People might not think this is hard, but when you start being honest with yourself and no longer blame others for your shortcomings, mistakes, and issues, you start to see what honesty is all about! You learn that you must stop and consider the ramifications of your actions before you do them. You must stop and think about the effect of your words before you open your mouth.

I finally came to the realization that past abuses and other situations I had been through were the reason for my problems. But I also realized what happened in my past wasn't my present problem. As they say, "The problem is never the problem." The real problem— the cause of the visible symptoms—was lurking beneath the surface.

So how are you doing in the area of self-awareness and honesty? Have you become more aware of your shortcomings? If you have, what are they?

1. _____

2. _____

3. _____
_____

4. _____

5. _____

Are you making less excuses for yourself? The only way to achieve honesty with yourself is to quit making excuses, take the responsibility for your own words and actions, and begin to change the way you talk and react.

Counselor and Support Team

Are you satisfied with your support team? Are there any changes you would like to make? Be careful not to make any hasty adjustments without first consulting your counselor or pastor. I know that depending on a support team for honest feedback will probably be hard at first because of the human tendency to run away from someone who truly wants to help you. I know this all too well because I didn't want to face the very people who were trying to help me. It almost cost me my life! Had I not come to my senses when I did, I wouldn't have made it. Thank God for His grace and mercy! So let me encourage you to stick with your support team, and you will grow and excel.

Family and Friends

What about certain friends or family members? Have you concluded that you would make better progress on your healing journey if you walked away from them or at least limited the time you spend with them? Are you still hanging around people who are hindering your progress—pushing you toward negative behavior or the lifestyle you are trying to leave behind?

These are some hard questions, but they must be looked at and followed through. I had to walk away from a few people in my life. It was very hard because I was a people-pleaser and they wouldn't take no for an answer. I had to learn that I could love people without doing what they wanted me to do. It was more important to please God.

Journaling

Journaling is an excellent way to track your progress. You think you will remember everything that happened on your healing journey, but trust me, you won't. It's very important to journal about everything—both your bad days as well as your good ones. I was greatly helped and encouraged when I turned back the pages and recognized how far I had come and the many things God had done in my life!

Turn back the pages of your journal. Can you see how much you have grown and changed for the better? If so, write about it in the space provided below.

1. _____

2. _____

3. _____

4. _____

5. _____

6. _____

Take note of some of your bad days. Isn't it thrilling to see that you have overcome some of those behaviors? Name some specific areas in which you see improvement or which you have overcome:

1. _____

2.
_____

3. _____

4. _____

5. _____

6. _____

I am so proud and happy for you. Thank God for bringing so much healing to your spirit and mind!

Repentance

Have you allowed yourself to be broken before God so He can look inside your heart in those very deep places? That is a necessary—and wonderful—start on your healing journey. Are you repenting every day? Paul said, "I die daily." We must keep this up if we intend to go through the process and complete the journey. As you do this, God will continue to speak to you and help you to see the areas that need work. Let me remind you that you should repent about something only once. If you continue to repent over the same thing(s), it will lead to depression. God hears you the first time and then chooses not to remember your sins anymore. God is faithful and just to forgive.

Forgiveness

Have you forgiven every person who has wronged you in the past? If you have truly let God break you, forgiveness will not be hard, especially when you recognize the huge filthy heap of things God has forgiven you for. Sometimes as you work through the process of healing you will all of a sudden realize you are holding a certain person responsible for his/her actions or words that hurt you. You didn't even realize you needed to forgive them! That's all right; that is how this is supposed to work. God doesn't allow you to see everything at once because you would be overwhelmed. There is a time and place for everything—even for forgiving someone, especially if it's a person who has abused you. God's timing is perfect. If you still have more to do in this area, I encourage you to take your time and walk methodically through the process. It will make you free indeed!

Can you think of some people you have forgiven? Write their names on the lines below.

1. _____

2. _____

3. _____

4. _____

5. _____

6. _____

Great job! It's a wonderful feeling to know you have forgiven these people and now you can move on. Are there others you still need to forgive and deal with? Write these down.

1. _____

2. _____

3. _____

4. _____

5. _____

6. _____

My prayer is that God will help you as you make progress in this area of forgiveness. Keep your heart open and clear as there probably are more people God wants to bring to your mind that need your forgiveness. You can do it. God is well pleased when you forgive because you are exhibiting one of His loveliest attributes.

Restitution

Are you making progress in the area of restitution? Or haven't you started yet? This area of my journey took a lot of time because there were so many people I had to contact, and because I had to reach a certain level of healing before I had the strength to make restitution. My counselor, Vani Marshall, and my pastor, Stan Gleason, kindly helped me work through this process.

Your progress in the area of restitution may take a little extra time as well, depending on your personal situation. It may not be evident at first exactly what you need to do in order to right your wrongs. Once you have apologized, you must be willing to make restitution where necessary. This is a vital part of your healing journey, so don't back away from it.

This was probably one of the hardest things I have ever had to do. It was both grueling and devastating. It crumpled every shred of pride I had left. I had to eat a veritable banquet of words, and believe me, they are never good the second time around.

There is a silver lining, however. Making restitution will earn people's respect. They see you are willing to go the extra mile in order to make everything right. I assure you that good people will not look down on you for apologizing and making restitution. But they will if you balk and refuse to make things right.

I encourage you to keep making progress in this area, even if it moves slowly. Once you have unloaded the huge bag of "trespasses," the lightness and freedom you feel in your spirit will be well worth the effort! I believe you can do it. You are more than a conqueror through Him who loves you!

Your Identity

Are you keeping up with your Bible-reading every day, or at least more days than not? Failure to hide the Word of God in your heart could sabotage your healing journey. The more you read the Bible the more your new identity will emerge. Remember to track your progress in this area so as time passes you will recognize the new person you have become in Christ. You will see it and you will feel it. You will recognize yourself as God's child. You will gain self-respect and confidence. You will be able to see your great qualities and talents.

Here is a list of some things I started seeing in myself as my healing journey progressed:

1. Less fear.
2. More courage.
3. More confidence.

4. I knew I was God's child.
5. I felt His presence more.
6. I felt closer to God.
7. I would perform tasks I couldn't do before.

How are you doing in the area of your identity in Christ? Can you see any improvement? Are there some good things you see in yourself that you did not see before?

1. _____

2. _____

3. _____

4. _____

5. _____

6. _____

How do you feel about your body image? Are you feeling comfortable with the way God made you? Do you know and believe God makes no mistakes? Here are some things I discovered about myself in the area of body image:

1. My body will not always be slim and trim.
2. It's okay to have thin hair.
3. It's okay that my nose is a little crooked.
4. It's okay that I don't have slim, pretty feet.

What are some details about your body that you have learned to accept?

1. _____

2. _____

3. _____

4. _____

5. _____

6. _____

     I encourage you to come back to every area in this chapter as many times as you need to so you can track your progress. You will be surprised at how far you have come. I hope you have already made progress while reading this book and started putting into practice some of the disciplines and steps of healing. If you have made only a little improvement, be patient with yourself and give yourself time to work on them. Then come back for another review.

Prayer

     Are you praying every day? Are you spending a little longer with God as you move through each day? Do you feel closer to Him? One thing I learned in my prayer time was this: I don't have to be overcome with emotion to have a good prayer time. I had always put plenty of emotion into my prayers. The more emotion the better the prayer, right? Wrong. Did all of the emotion repair my relationships? Did it spur me to admit I needed help? Did it lead me to repent of the things I was harboring? Did it plant the seed of the Word of God in my heart? No. The truth is, after I started the process of healing all of the steps began working together and I began to accept my true identity in Christ. I began to look forward to my daily communion with God. It was no longer a duty. I learned I could talk to Him just like I talk to my friends. I don't have to raise my voice. I don't have to be melodramatic.

What have you learned in your prayer time?

1. _____

2. _____

3. _____

4. _____

5. _____

6. _____

The Word of God

After discovering my true identity in Christ, I started enjoying my Bible-reading. The Bible came alive! One of the Bible verses that spoke to me was Philippians 4:13: "I can do all things through Christ who strengthens me." I had read this verse umpteen times before and believed it. But when I started seeing the healing God was accomplishing in me and how He was helping me do things I didn't think I could do, and giving me strength when I thought I was at my weakest, this verse spoke volumes!

As you read your Bible, what verse(s) seems to speak to you?

1. _____

2. _____

3. _____

4._____

5. _____

God can help you through anything—even things you think are impossible!

Taking Every Thought Captive

Are you learning to corral your wandering thoughts? If they were always chasing each other around in your head, is the pace starting to slow down? This is a hard thing to do, but as you learn to

179

take every thought captive it will lower your stress level. You will begin to take control of your mind.

Racing thoughts are a torment! I remember those days all too well. Maybe you, along with many others, are suffering from it as well. But as you begin to "think on these things," God will help you! Think on things that are true, honest, just, pure, lovely, virtuous, praiseworthy, and of a good report. You can learn to control what you think about. You can learn to give God your burdens.

What thoughts are you turning over to God?

1. _____

2. _____

3. _____

4. _____

5. _____

6. _____

By now you've probably realized how much time you've wasted thinking about things that weren't worth thinking. Worrying leads to nonproductive living. I will say that as time goes on and you learn to take every thought captive, your thoughts will slow down and you'll be able to examine them in the light of God's Word. This was one of the first things I noticed. It was such a relief. It also freed up other areas of my brain, and I was able to accomplish more.

What thoughts are you still allowing to run crazily through your mind that you need to take captive?

1. _____

2. _____

3. _____

4. _____

5. _____

6. _____

Don't hesitate to write these thoughts on paper. It will make you more aware of them and thus easier to capture. Probably more than ninety percent of what we worry about never happens anyway. What a waste of time and mental energy!

Don't let this area discourage you. Some days will be much easier, especially days when your schedule is not loaded with activity. But hectic schedules or unexpected crises can throw you into a tailspin. Just be patient; this too shall pass. Tomorrow will be a better day. You can do this. God will see you through!

The Spoken Word

The spoken Word of God is powerful! Some days you just have to speak out the Word and claim it in order to get the victory over the enemy.

Thank God for your healing every day! Claim it every day. Speak those things that are not as though they were. The spoken Word builds your faith. When you listen to a testimony of God's healing power, think about how God can do it for you too. This book is my testimony. If God did it for me, He can do it for you! On those days when your spirit is down, claim the power of God in your life and in your spirit. Keep a positive outlook. God is the answer to your prayer!

Grounding and Focusing

How are you doing in the area of grounding and focusing? You have to consistently work at the exercises offered in this book in order to improve. Make note of the exercises that have been the greatest help in the midst of a crisis or a bump in the road.

1. _____

2. _____

3. _____

     The exercise I used most was Slow Deep Breathing from chapter 14. In addition, I also used strong scents when I dissociated. Smelling a strong scent would capture my attention and bring my thoughts back to where I could sort them out. An analogy would be a customer walking into a store and smelling a beautiful aroma. She says, "Wow! That smells good!"

     If you are having problems with grounding and focusing, don't let it stress you or get you down. Keep experimenting until you find the exercises that help you most, or revise them to meet your needs. You don't have to do them exactly as outlined. Sometimes doing an activity that forces you to focus will help you collect yourself. My strategy was cooking. Cooking helped me focus on the here-and-now and brought my mind back to where it needed to be. Activities that require focus and concentration—like following a recipe and preparing food—help you refocus and bring all of your thoughts back to one place.

     As you continue to heal, you will begin to need these exercises less and less. You will have less trouble bringing your mind back to the present while sitting in a roomful of people, simply by doing some deep breathing exercises. Don't be afraid to try different things like going shopping or taking a trip to the lake to watch the water. You will find your niche.

     As you go through your healing journey, come back to this chapter as many times as you need to and see how far you have come. I recommend, however, that you let at least a couple weeks go by before tracking your progress. It will give you hope when you look back and see how far you and God have come!

Chapter 16

Bursting Alive

Therefore, if anyone is in Christ, he is a new creation; old things have passed away; behold, all things have become new. (II Corinthians 5:17)

We use this Scripture verse in the context of when someone is born again of water and Spirit and begins to live a life pleasing to God. But this verse has an additional meaning for me. After walking through my miracle journey of healing, I feel like a totally different person. My mind has been transformed. I know who I am in Christ. I'm living an abundant life. I am a new creature in Christ!

All my life I have heard testimonies about the change that comes to people when Jesus touches their lives and makes them whole. We marvel at the amazing stories of alcoholics or drug addicts or gang members whose eyes are opened to the truth. They repent, get baptized in Jesus' name, and receive the Holy Ghost. We celebrate this greatest of miracles with them. I thank God for all the newborn babes in Christ!

But in my humble opinion, I think we should celebrate miracles of emotional and/or mental healing of someone who has been attempting to walk with God the best they know how through all the hurt, pain, and baggage they've been carrying. To me it is just as great a miracle when the power of God guides a person down the road of renewal, and, through His grace, rewires their mind and thinking. We don't celebrate this kind of miracle as much as we should.

I believe through experience that when we first receive the Holy Spirit it cleans our spirit, but we still must contend with our mind and emotions. If a child receives the Holy Spirit at a young age and lives in an unhealthy environment, there will be problems. As a side note, we all live in some form or degree of dysfunction. Nobody's home is perfect. We all live in a fallen world and must contend with our carnal nature. Some don't get to choose the best route or the best exit ramps on life's highway.

Have you ever been traveling along an unfamiliar route? Let's say you are zipping along an interstate highway when all of a sudden one of the passengers needs to make a pit stop. So you start looking for that perfect convenience store. You scan the signs as you pass by to see what is available at each exit. When the person with the problem gets impatient, you say, "Okay, I'm going to pull off at the next exit. Surely we'll find someplace there." You cruise down the exit ramp, look both ways—and see absolutely nothing! Which way should you turn? You decide to turn right. You travel down the road looking for a gas station or store. Nothing. Everyone in the car becomes frustrated, especially the person who has to go. The road has led to nowhere! You've wasted precious time that you really didn't have. You make a U-turn, get back on the interstate, and continue to drive. You say, "I'm not doing that again! I will stay on this interstate until I come to a good exit—one I know for sure has the facilities we need."

As we travel through life, many of us have taken many wrong turns, some intentional, some unintentional. At times we had no control at all; maybe we happened to be a passenger and the driver made a bad choice. Although we were totally innocent, we suffered from the wrong choice along with everyone else. Has this happened to you? Have you been in the car as the driver exited life's highway and turned into a dead end road? You thought you would never find your way back—or maybe you didn't know where they made the wrong turn in the first place!

Some people who have taken wrong roads in life didn't stay on them very long and were able to get back on the right highway and reverse any damage that occurred. But there are others who aren't aware that they've taken a wrong turn, and because of it, they continue to drive on the wrong road, creating and accumulating a large amount of collateral damage that may take some time to fix. It depends on how far they went before discovering they were headed in the wrong direction.

I was one who didn't know I was going the wrong direction. I had absolutely no clue. Not only had I got off on the wrong exit, I kept going until I was lost in a wasteland! Windstorms filled my eyes with sand, blinding me. I couldn't see where I was going. But the grace of God was shining down on me. God looked beyond my fault and saw my need!

For me, the healing road was long and hard. That's why I say when a Spirit-filled Christian receives this type of healing it is as great a miracle as a person who is a newborn babe in Christ. I now have an abundance of grace and mercy for others who have been traveling the wrong highway and fallen prey to addictions, disorders, and emotional problems. If this is you, and you're wondering if you'll ever get to the place where Jodie Smith is in her miracle, the answer is *yes, you will!* But in order to make the U-turn back toward recovery, you must be able to hear God speaking to you, telling you that your thinking process is wrong.

Is God showing you that some of your thoughts are wrong? Which ones?

1. _____

2. _____

3. _____

4. _____

5. _____

6. _____

I want you to ponder these thoughts and pray about them. Ask God to open your eyes to *all* wrong thinking. If you have a counselor and/or support team, be willing to listen to what they have to say about your thinking. You have to have an open mind. You can do it!

Once you start to see where you are thinking wrong, your condition will begin to make sense to you. You will start to see a pattern in your thinking. For instance, maybe you will discover that your feeling of being unloved is the root of your hypersensitivity and unwillingness to accept love. This causes you to reject people who are trying to tell you, "I love you!"

The above paragraph is just one example that might trigger a memory of other wrong thinking patterns you have and have not yet realized. Don't be afraid to ask someone close to you who loves you

185

to be honest with you, and to tell you what they see in your thinking that might need to be changed.

There have been so many positive changes in my life that it's hard to know where to even begin! I feel like the person who wrote the song "Amazing Grace": "I once was lost but now I'm found." I am a brand new person, and upon waking every day, I thank God for my miracle healing!

You see, if you know a Borderline or have read anything about the disorder, you will know they don't *ever* admit that they are doing wrong! *Never!* Most Borderlines go to their grave never knowing they were a Borderline. Until the end they think everybody else is at fault, not them. That's why I say my first miracle was being able to see that my thinking was wrong.

Recognizing that you are not thinking correctly is the first step toward healing. Let Jesus open your eyes to the truth, because "ye shall know the truth, and the truth shall make you free" (John 8:32, KJV)! When you receive this truth, it is your first step toward a complete miracle.

I want you to understand that in cases like this God heals you "precept upon precept . . . line upon line; here a little and there a little" (Isaiah 28:10). The healing process in your mind is slow and steady. It is happening every day, but you don't realize it until after some time has passed and you look back to reflect on how far you have come. Every day you must keep up with the strategies mentioned in this book such as prayer, Bible reading, counseling, and—one of the hardest—working at changing your thinking process. God will help you, but you must do your part. It's not an easy road, but it will be worth it.

I have no more depression in my life. I am truly happy and have an unspeakable joy inside. What a transformation from my former life! I used to be plagued with depression and suicidal thoughts. My normal everyday thinking was, "Nobody needs me." "I don't matter!" But I was mistaken. The truth all along was that my family and friends did need me! I did matter! I was a child of God! I had royal blood flowing through my veins! Knowing the truth has freed me of feeling like I don't matter. I am a new creature in Christ!

I would have to say the number-one difference in my life is a sound, clear, and free mind. If you have never experienced racing thoughts, you are blessed. They depleted my energy until at night I was exhausted. Our minds were not created to think that way. God created us to go to Him with our cares, needs, and burdens. Having racing thoughts causes anxiety and stress, which in turn causes many illnesses to occur in our bodies. Our bodies simply cannot handle it. I thank God every day for a sound mind—the mind He created me to have. As thoughts come one at a time, I can take them captive and weigh them against the Word of God to see if they are right, pure, and holy. If they are not, I banish them immediately from my mind.

I get so excited writing about this because it was such a transformation. My whole thought process has moved to the right track. It has been revised and regrouped. My judgments are now based on facts. That in itself was a new thought process for me, because a Borderline bases conclusions on emotions. This is why they are constantly switching back and forth with what they think and say. Our emotions lie to us sometimes. Yes, emotion still plays a role in my conclusions about any given situation, but I am able to be led by facts and can explain why I arrived at my answer.

My life is free of hypersensitivity and suspicion. These two things alone can lead one into trouble. My thoughts are no longer self-centered (i.e., how I feel and how everything affects me). When you take *me* out of the picture and look at how things affect your loved ones and others around you, it changes your thinking patterns. It changes your life.

All of this came into play in my healing process. If God had changed my thinking in one split second, I would have been profoundly shocked and lost. I wouldn't have known what to do, how to react, or even how to survive. God gave me time in this area so I could reflect on questions like "Who am I?" "What am I doing?" As time went on I was a stranger to myself. It was as if I had shed my old life and left it lying on the wrong road. I am a new person—healed and whole! God has totally transformed my mind!

As any newborn babe in Christ must learn how to think and act "Christianly," I had to learn a new thought process, which in turn gave me a whole new way of reacting to things. My responses were transformed as well as my mind. I could respond in a Christlike way to something that I normally would have taken very personally and counterattacked with words or walked away hurt, angry, and upset. I could now respond differently because I realized it was said in love; it was intended to help, not put down. It is such a blessing to have conversations with people and not think everyone is out to get me. It's amazing how God can take a hopeless situation and make it turn out for the good.

Inconsistency is another significant area in which God has brought healing to me. I will say there is a difference between someone with a personality that tends to be unorganized and in occasional disarray and Borderlines. Borderlines are inconsistent in everything they do! It drives their friends crazy, not to mention their spouse and family. They are constantly changing their answer or opinion. They are unorganized simply because their minds are in chaos. They are very forgetful. I used to make a list so I wouldn't forget important things and events, but it didn't help because I forgot I even made a list to begin with! Inconsistency stems from a horribly skewed thinking pattern. Racing thoughts and churned-up emotions make it impossible for a Borderline to be consistent.

My healed mind has become much more consistent. I'm not perfect by any means, but it's such a relief to be back to a normal life, the life God created me to live. I no longer worry about all the things I might have forgotten or left out. Sure, I still may forget a few things here and there, but compared to how I used to be, it is of no consequence. This has helped me to feel much more confident and secure. I have been made whole. I am not running around brainless, like a chicken with my head cut off!

I saw some beheaded chickens one time. My grandmother had come to our house for a visit right around the time my brother decided he no longer wanted to take care of his chickens. So my grandmother was assigned the task of putting them down. I had heard the saying, "running around like a chicken with your head cut off," but I hadn't realize that they literally do! I remember as a little girl being shocked and horrified to see them running and flopping crazily around the yard for a minute or two, headless. Through hindsight, I realize that was an apt picture of my life a good part of the time. Thank You, Jesus, I am not that way anymore!

Are you wanting to experience the same healing that God did for me? What are some of your thoughts? Write them in the space provided below.

1. _____

2. _____

3. _____

4. _____

5. _____

6. _____

What are some of the ways in which you conduct your life every day that you would like to see changed?

1. _____

2. _____

3. _____

4. _____

5. _____

6. _____

I want to encourage you that you can receive your miracle too! God is no respecter of persons. All you have to have is a little faith—no larger than the size of a mustard seed. Believing is the first step to receiving what God has for you!

Don't let the enemy prey upon your mind. I believe the devil goes about like a roaring lion searching for people who are not whole in their mind because they are easy prey. Just as a lion will pick on the young, the weak, and the elderly, the devil will stalk the weak-minded and move in for the kill.

Not only that, if we harbor anger, it's the same as leaving a foothold in our mind for Satan's attacks. This is why the Bible says in Ephesians 4:26, "'Be angry and do not sin': do not let the sun go down on your wrath." In other words, don't go to bed angry because it leaves a foothold for Satan. Borderlines think negatively anyway, and it's very easy for them to be influenced by the devil. I found this out the hard way, but praise God I have a sound mind and am much more aware when Satan comes around and tries to distract me. I can now say, "Get thee behind me, Satan." I plead the blood of Jesus over my mind every day.

What a great blessing it is to know God is with me at all times and I am His child. I feel secure in His presence. I am not easily deceived and turned around. I am aware and can take every thought captive. I find security in His Word.

I have set healthy boundaries: I know who I am. I no longer have to be a people pleaser. I don't have to wear a mask. I can please God and still love people! A people pleaser is an unhappy person. They are constantly wondering if this one or that one is upset or unhappy with them. But if you are pleasing God, that's all that matters. You cannot make everybody happy all of the time. Just because some people get upset when you don't respond to them like they want you to does not mean you have done something wrong. It may be they wanted a compliment in order for them to feel good about themselves. Some people are constantly fishing for compliments, but that's not why you offer them. You give compliments when you truly think they did a great job at something or they look really nice in what they chose to wear, for example.

When we are healthy, we can set healthy boundaries. We will feel so much better about ourselves. We will not walk away feeling like people are taking advantage of us. I found that to be true after my healing. I could quickly pick up on unhealthy conversation. I have learned how to walk away politely. Stinking thinking isn't good for anyone.

I now can pick and choose the friends and people I want to be with—not that I think I am better than anyone else; I just can't afford to feel that gravitational pull toward negativity. I would rather spend time with people and groups that talk about uplifting things, and when I walk away, I feel renewed and refreshed in my spirit. You tend to take on the thought patterns, opinions, language, and actions of the people with whom you spend the most time, so I prefer to be with people who are like the person I would like to become.

I thank God for the people He has placed in my life, some of whom stayed only a short time in order to help me in a certain area and then moved on to help someone else. Then there are those who have been in my life forever. They are still there, lending support and love through thick and thin.

My walk with God has changed because now I know who He really is. I know He is my heavenly Father. I know He is ever present in the time of trouble and will give me strength to overcome whatever situation I'm facing. I feel closer to Him because my mind is not crammed with thousands of thoughts. I no long am trying to do and figure out everything on my own.

I have found a new and great way to live. I no longer do things out of duty or a ritual but because I truly love my God. I have a much greater capacity to love than I had before. I thought I loved before, but after the miracle healing touch, I have learned I cannot love anyone else if I don't love myself. I'm so glad I have found a love better than life itself! I treasure the love I have found. I can now feel the love everyone has toward me. I believe them when they say, "I love you."

I can accept compliments from people and respond, "Thank you!" Do you know people who cannot accept a compliment? Commenting on something nice they have said or done makes them uncomfortable, as if they don't know what to say, do, or how to act. They can't accept it because they don't think they deserve it. They don't love themselves.

God created you with a desire for words of affirmation and encouragement. He gives them to you over and over again in His Word. He has wonderful thoughts about you. Can you accept them? If it is hard for you to accept compliments and encouraging words from others, you won't be able to receive them from God either.

I can walk upright with a sound mind and with confidence knowing He is still doing a work in me and will not stop working until I walk on the streets of gold. He will never give up on me. He has patience and forgiveness that never runs out.

With a healed mind you can do so much more and even see new ways to minister to others you never dreamed yourself capable of. For instance, I had no idea that I would write a book. Who would have ever dreamed I would be an author—that God could speak to others through the words that I type upon these pages? God can do much more work through you when you have a healed mind. The possibilities are endless.

God is in the miracle-working business. If He did it for me, He will do it for you. Don't let yourself give up. You will fall, but that is a given. There is nothing wrong with falling, but something *is* wrong if you just lie there. You must get back up and keep walking and trying. Keep your mind open each day to what God is teaching you. You are growing every day whether or not you feel it or see it. I believe in you because I believe in God!

Chapter 17

You Are Valuable

I want to end this book with this message: you are valuable! You may have been hurt, bruised, and battered, but regardless of your story, you are valuable.

> For you created my inmost being; you knit me together in my mother's womb. I praise you because I am fearfully and wonderfully made; your works are wonderful, I know that full well. My frame was not hidden from you when I was made in the secret place. When I was woven together in the depths of the earth, your eyes saw my unformed body. All the days ordained for me were written in your book before one of them came to be. How precious to me are your thoughts, Oh God! How vast is the sum of them! Were I to count them, they would outnumber the grains of sand. When I awake, I am still with you. (Psalm 139:13–18, NIV)

The inspiration for this chapter was a sermon my husband preached called "I Am Valuable." Every single person God has created is valuable. God does not make junk! This means you are unique and special; according to I Peter 2:9 (KJV), you are "peculiar":

> But you are a chosen generation, a royal priesthood, an holy nation, a peculiar people; that ye should shew forth the praises of him who hath called you out of darkness into his marvellous light.

What do you think of when you hear the word *peculiar*? Some would say it means odd, weird, or different, but that is not what the word means in this verse. *Peculiar*, according to the *Expository Dictionary of New Testament Words* by W. E. Vine, simply means "purchased treasure"; the *Complete Word Study Dictionary New*

Testament by Spiros Zodhiates Th.D. says "a people acquired or purchased to Himself in a peculiar or unique manner." We are snug in His embrace and guarded closely because He paid a tremendous price for us. We are special and precious to Him.

You probably have read I Peter 2:9 and/or heard it preached many times, but has the understanding of its implications really sunk into your spirit? Have you accepted the reality of it? You are God's valuable treasure!

When a woman gives birth and the newborn is placed into her arms, she is instantly in love with her baby. It is so precious to her! Elated, she quickly inspects its ten fingers and ten toes. Her husband is standing there smiling from ear to ear at the precious child who soon will be calling him "Daddy," and he is smitten with a deep love and a desire to protect this little one.

There is no love like parental love. Parents will go the extra mile to make sure their little one has everything it needs. No other human can possess as much love for a baby as its mom and dad. God spent six days creating a beautiful and amazing universe, but He labored nine months creating you in your mother's womb. No wonder you are so special to Him. You represent nine months of thought and creativity. Imagine how much it must grieve the heart of God when He goes back to put some special touches on His creation and it's gone. The baby has been aborted. The treasure He loves and created has been sucked out and discarded as if it were a piece of garbage.

When a child is born into the world, I imagine He loves to see all the oohing and admiring over His special creation. I am sure it warms His heart to look at the baby's beautiful black hair and sweet chubby cheeks. Many of us have experienced the fierce love inspired by the births of our own children but still have trouble knowing and accepting that God loves us that much and more. Moms and dads give their kids more chances and more benefit of the doubt than anyone else. As a mother, I could come up with many excuses for why my kids did the things they did or misbehaved at times. They are a part of me. They contain my genes. That's pretty remarkable.

Let this truth of how much God loves you roll over in your mind and be absorbed deep into your heart. You are so precious to Him! In His family there are no big I's and little you's; we are all equally special in God's eyes. I'll admit that some mothers or fathers have been known to favor one of their children over the others. There

194

is a biblical example of this in the life of Jacob, who favored his son Joseph over his other sons. His special affection for Joseph was evident to all the other children, since Jacob gave his favorite son a coat of many colors. This created hatred and jealously in the hearts of Joseph's brothers. But God does not do things like that. He is fair and just. He doesn't pick and choose only the elite, the well-educated, the rich, or the professionals. In God's eyes we are all His children, all equally loved.

It is wonderful to know that God did not end His work in me on the day of my birth. While I was still in the womb, He planned out what He wanted for my life! Psalm 139:16 (NIV) says, "All the days ordained for me were written in your book before one of them came to be." This is why we should put so much emphasis on finding and obeying the will of God. I want to perform what God had in mind for me when He created me. Jesus said, "Whoever does God's will is my brother and sister and mother" (Mark 3:35, NIV). We must not only be thankful and accept God's creation of us, but we must also seek His will for our life and pursue it.

Do you know what God's will is for your life? Write down what you think it is.

_____

_____

Is it hard for you to believe that God has an awesome plan for your life? Do you feel you have no value? Why?

1. _____

2. _____

3. _____

4. _____

5. _____

6. _____

The fact that God had everything planned out before you were born shows His tender love for you. "For I know the thoughts that I think toward you, saith the LORD, thoughts of peace, and not of evil, to give you an expected end" (Jeremiah 29:11, KJV).

You are valuable, so please don't abort the plans God has for you. All your life you must be in submission to His will. Will you understand everything God has planned? No. "For my thoughts are not your thoughts, neither are your ways my ways, saith the LORD. For as the heavens are higher than the earth, so are my ways higher than your ways, and my thoughts than your thoughts" (Isaiah 55:8–9, KJV).

So please be aware that although God will reveal His will to you, He will not show you all the steps and stages of the plan at once. I'm sure there were many times in your life when you thought you had it all figured out. You thought you knew where God was taking you. Then after the fact, you looked back and everything played out much differently than you expected. You say, "I didn't see that coming. I can't believe it happened that way!" His ways are higher than our ways, and His thoughts are higher than our thoughts. God can see the end from the beginning. This alone should let us know His plan will be different than ours.

> If you took a fifty dollar bill out of your pocket and threw it on the floor, its value would still be fifty dollars. If you threw that fifty dollar bill in the trash, its value would still be fifty dollars. If you put that fifty dollar bill on the floor and stomped it until it had a thousand wrinkles or until it had a tear or maybe until it was torn in half, its worth would still be fifty dollars! (Scott Smith sermon, "You Are Valuable")

You may feel as if you've been thrown away, rejected, and left for dead, but you still have the same value. You may have been sexually, physically, mentally, or emotionally abused, but you are still valuable! Your mother may not have wanted you or been able to care for you and you ended up in the foster-care system. You are still valuable.

While we were pastoring, one of our church members had a child due to a date rape. She valued that child the same as her other children because God created him and had a plan for his life. No matter what family you were born into, God created you, placed great value on you, and designed a master plan for your life!

Remember God is capable of bringing good out of everything, no matter what the situation is. The deciding factor is if you will allow Him to work. Are you allowing God to make and mold you? Are you allowing Him to bring good out of everything bad that happens in your life? Are you following His will?

Think of your life as having two ships: one is loaded with victories and successes; the other is filled with defeats, failures, mistakes, and shortcomings. Both of these ships contain valuable cargo. We like to sort through our great victories and successes and talk about those good times and how much they mean to us—because that is our favorite ship. It's the other ship we struggle with. Who wants to sort through the failures and shortcomings of their life? That would be like sailing into a sinkhole of depression, right? Not if we learn to allow God to bring good out of our bad. Part of how He does this is teaching us to forgive and make restitution to those we have wronged and then use the experiences for good.

We can learn how to turn our failures into a testimony of God's grace and mercy that will help and encourage someone else. We will encounter many people in similar situations that we could influence to take their past mistakes and failures and turn them into victories! When they see where God has brought us from, it gives them hope that maybe God can do it for them too!

> Brethren, I count not myself to have apprehended: but this one thing I do, forgetting those things which are behind, and reaching forth unto those things which are before, I press toward the mark for the prize of the high calling of God in Christ Jesus. (Philippians 3:13–14, KJV)

We must press forward into the future that God has for us. He has ordered our steps. Our past, both good experiences and bad, has brought us to where we are today, but while past events are important, they do not define who we are. We get our identity through Jesus Christ.

I want you to take a minute and visualize yourself healed and whole. What would you like to see in your future?

1. _____

2. _____

3. _____

4. _____

5. _____

6. _____

The Scripture says you can do all things through Christ who strengthens you. What things are you having trouble doing that you know God wants you to do but you can't because you're being hindered by past hurts and wounds?

1. _____

2. _____

3. _____

4. _____

5. _____

I want to encourage you that all things are possible with God. With God in your life every day, you can make it. You can eat and breathe God! Acts 17:28 says you live and move and have your being in Him. You are valuable and God has healing in store for you. I'm convinced of this because it's always God's will for His children to be whole in mind and body. If you are wondering if God will heal you too, of course He will. You just have to be willing to work with Him, going through the steps of healing outlined in this book, and working as you've never worked before to get the result you want to experience. I believe in you and God believes in you! You can receive your healing through the power of Jesus Christ!

Chapter 18

Understanding Motivation
By Scott Breedlove

"Optimism is the faith that leads to achievement. Nothing can be done without hope and confidence." – Helen Keller

What causes a teenager to clean up his room and tell his mom how much he loves her? Perhaps he is setting her up to say yes when he comes to her later and asks to spend the night with a friend. What causes a professional within an organization make another coworker look bad on a project? Perhaps she believes that the coworker is her toughest competition for an upcoming promotion. What causes Dorothy from the Wizard of Oz to face her fears and put her life at risk to kill the wicked witch of the west? We know the answer to this question is that she has a desire to go home and needs the witch's broom to do so. People do things for a reason. The reason or reasons can be thought of as motivation for a behavior.

One definition of the word *motivation* is "the reason or reasons one has for acting or behaving in a particular way." People can be motivated by an unlimited number of reasons. An argument can be made that motivation works around the clock twenty-four hours a day, day after day, influencing us to do things. Motivation can be viewed as intrinsic or extrinsic, meaning some motivation comes from within us (intrinsic) or motivation can come from outside sources (extrinsic). While extrinsic motivation can be helpful in starting a change process, intrinsic motivation becomes important for individuals to create new thoughts and behaviors and to sustain long-term changes in their life.

Individuals with Borderline Personality Disorder are not exempt from motivation. There are reasons for the words they say and the behavior they exhibit, and while the reasons may seem natural and make perfect sense for the individual, they are distorted by the disorder and can create conflict with those closest to the person with BPD. Understanding the specific motivational factors driving their behavior and reviewing these factors through the lens of God's Word can spark a light of hope within an individual to find the courage to seek help and begin the journey of healing and recovery.

God is interested in motivation. Second Corinthians 9:7 (KJV) says, "Every man according as he purposeth in his heart, so let him give; not grudgingly, or of necessity: for God loveth a cheerful giver." This verse explains to us that God is looking beyond the act of giving but is looking into the heart of the reason why a person is giving. In fact, Scripture is clear that Jesus may have been the most motivated person to ever walk the earth. His birth, His life, and His death were focused on one goal. Hebrews 12:2 (KJV) says, "Who for the joy that was set before him endured the cross, despising the shame, and is set down at the right hand of the throne of God." Luke 19:10 (KJV) states, "For the Son of man is come to seek and to save that which was lost."

As a person with BPD begins to heal and recover, God can begin to peel back the curtain of motivation to expose deep-rooted traumas that have created thought patterns that result in behaviors motivated by cognitive distortions and irrational perceptions of reality. Allowing yourself to be open and vulnerable and doing the work of self-examination and self-realization begins to impact the intrinsic motivation of understanding who you are as a person, recognizing your true value as a child of God, and implementing thoughts and behaviors to accomplish what God has in mind for you.

Exercise 1:
People are often motivated by what has happened in their past and more specifically how they perceive and process the events in their life. For instance, a person who grew up very poor may be motivated to buy as much as they can as an adult because they didn't have much growing up. However, another person who grew up poor may be motivated to save as much as they can and not spend to ensure their protection due to a feeling of lack of safety in growing up poor and perhaps having to move a lot or not having basic necessities of life. In looking back at your past, think about the events of your life and list the most important factors that have shaped your motivational decision-making model.

1. _____

2. _____

3. _____

4. _____

5. _____

Exercise 2:
Spend time thinking and journaling about how these motivational factors could interfere with your relationship with God. Do these factors align with biblical principles? Do they help you better reflect the image of Christ? For instance, does the motivation behind how you handle your finances cause you to overspend and create debt that interferes with your ability to fulfill God's calling on your life, or does your over-saving rob you of the ability to give to the kingdom of God through missions and other endeavors and change lives, possibly for eternity?

For individuals with BPD, close relationships are hard to cultivate and maintain. The negative self-image and fear of abandonment cause the individual to self-sabotage the relationship. The struggle to trust and believe that your friend or spouse or someone else close to you likes and loves you for who you are will provide motivation to stay distant and limit communication so you won't be hurt as badly when you are abandoned, which you are sure is eventually going to happen. A step toward healing and recovery can begin with a day-to-day reminder of how much God loves you and is faithful to you. Verses like Hebrews 13:5, "I will never leave you, nor forsake you," give hope within you that God is faithful and will never abandon you, which can increase your ability to see the possibility of other relationships that can be built on a foundation of trust and faithfulness.

Exercise 3
Think of and list several other verses that describe the faithfulness and commitment of God to always be there for you:

1. _____

2. _____

3. _____

    As you meditate and think about these verses of Scripture, create in your mind thoughts that if God can love you like that and commit to you like that, then God can give the desire and ability for others close to you to love and commit to you like that.

    People with BPD tend to feel emotions very intensely and can go back and forth between extreme points of view and extreme emotional experiences. This can cause them to be extremely intimate and passionate with someone one moment and then a moment later not want to have anything to do with them. A person with BPD must become comfortable recognizing these extremes and when expressing them to the right team of helpers, can feel validated for these feelings without feeling judged. Validation without judgment allows the person to examine both extremes and the origin of each thought pattern. This can allow the person to move toward positive changes in the relationship through increased motivation and commitment toward stronger relationships. Having a team of helpers that can validate without judgment also reinforces the idea that people can be trusted and will remain faithful to you even when you express your extreme viewpoints.

    You have goals, but sometimes your BPD attempts to hinder you from reaching those goals. Your goals and behavior have a discrepancy. Use this exercise to review your behaviors, specifically how they are interfering with your goals.

Exercise 4:
Write down several goals you are trying to accomplish. This could be a ministry goal, a relationship goal, a career goal, or a family goal. Then think about and write down specific behaviors that are interfering with your goals. Finally, make a commitment to change those behaviors to align with your goals. For instance, you may have a goal of developing a healthy long-term relationship built on friendship over time but you are often too quick to rush into relationships and express feelings of love too soon. This behavior is actually at odds with the goal and so you must acknowledge the behavior and replace it with a behavior that aligns with your goal. This might include prayer for God to give you the power to control your

tongue to not tell someone you love them too soon but to be okay with allowing the relationship to grow slowly over time.

1. _____

2. _____

3. _____

4. _____

Motivation is a necessary ingredient for change. Motivation is constantly changing and is multidimensional. You must constantly remain aware of what and who you are allowing to influence you. Motivation is interactive and increases and decreases as you interact with the world around you. Change can be hard. It is often easier to keep doing what you have always done. But if you are reading this book, there is already a seed of motivation for change placed inside of you desiring to sprout and grow. I'm sure if you examine your past, you can be amazed regarding what you have endured and overcome. Focus on your strengths and believe that through God all things are possible.

Scott Breedlove has a Master of Science Degree in Addiction Studies and is the Assistant Director for the Missouri Credentialing Board. He is a Recognized Associate Alcohol and Drug Counselor, a Medication Assisted Recovery Specialist, and a Certified Peer Specialist. Breedlove has served as pastor of Landmark Church in Jefferson City, Missouri, for twelve years.

Acknowledgements

First and foremost, I want to thank my dear husband, Scott, for his uninterrupted loyalty to me. He encouraged me along the way as I was writing this book. He is my number-one fan and supporter.

Thank you, Vani Marshall, for supporting the writing of this second book. You have believed in me and let me know I could do this. I have cherished all of your, "I'm proud of you" statements. You have been a loyal and sweet friend to me.

Thank you, Stan Gleason, my pastor and shepherd, for your great support and kindness as I have worked on this book. Thank you for believing in me.

Thank you, Pat Bollmann, for all your hours of editing this book. You have taught me so much and your input has been invaluable. I look forward to more writing adventures with you.

Thanks to my family and the many friends who were so encouraging after the publishing of my first book with their glowing and kind reviews and remarks. Those gave me the extra strength and support to write this second book.

Thank you, JoLynn Mills (savvydesignsolutions@gmail.com) for a beautiful cover design for this book. I love it! You did a wonderful job.

Suggested Reading

The Angry Heart: Overcoming Borderline and Addictive Disorders by Joseph Santoro, PhD

The Wounded Heart: Hope for Adult Victims of Childhood Sexual Abuse by Dr. Dan B. Allender

I Hate You—Don't Leave Me: Understanding the Borderline Personality by Jerold J. Kreisman, MD, and Hal Straus

Stop Walking on Eggshells: Taking your life back when someone you care about has Borderline Personality Disorder by Paul T. Mason, MS, and Randi Kreger

Total Forgiveness by R. T. Kendall

Forgiveness: The Ultimate Miracle by Paul J. Meyer

Buried Alive: A Miracle Journey of Healing from Borderline Personality Disorder by Jodie Smith